McGRAW-HILL
SCIENCE

Macmillan/McGraw-Hill Edition

Cross Curricular Projects

GRADE 5

S0-ASD-010

Mc Graw Hill **Macmillan McGraw-Hill**

New York   Farmington

Macmillan/McGraw-Hill

*A Division of The **McGraw·Hill** Companies*

Copyright © Macmillan/McGraw-Hilll, a Division of the Educational and Professional
Publishing Group of The McGraw-Hill Companies, Inc.

All rights reserved. Permission granted to reproduce for use with McGRAW-HILL SCIENCE. No other use of this
material or parts thereof, including reproduction, distribution, or storage in an electronic database, permitted without
the prior written permission of the publisher, except as provided under the United States Copyright Act of 1976.

Macmillan/McGraw-Hill
Two Penn Plaza
New York, New York 10121

Printed in the United States of America
ISBN 0-02-280136-6 / 5
1 2 3 4 5 6 7 8 9 079 06 05 04 03 02 01

Table of Contents

About Alice Eastwood

Connection to Reading
Science helps you learn about the events that shaped the life of an important scientist.

Alice Eastwood played an important role in our knowledge of plants. Carefully read each paragraph. Write a cause or effect in the space provided.

A. Alice Eastwood was born in Toronto, Canada in 1859. When Alice's mother died, her father left Alice and her sister in the care of their uncle. It was with her uncle that Alice first showed an interest in becoming a naturalist. A naturalist is a person who studies nature by observing plants and animals. Alice spent countless hours exploring the structure of every plant in her uncle's garden.

Cause: _____
Effect: Alice began living with her uncle.

B. Alice's father had a hard time making a living. He came back to get his children from her uncle when Alice was eight, only to leave a short time later. In 1873, Alice joined her father in Denver to be with her family. Her father's business failed, but Alice worked hard and graduated from high school. In 1879, Alice took a job teaching school in the small Rocky Mountain town of Kiowa, Colorado.

Cause: Alice wanted to be with her family.
Effect: _____

C. In 1881, Alice began hiking through the Colorado mountains to collect flowers. At the time it was almost unheard of for a woman to explore in the wilderness by herself. Indeed, the hiking clothes Alice wore—long skirts, high-top shoes, and bustles—were better suited for a parlor than a rugged mountain trail. However, Alice had no choice. In the 1880s, it was considered improper for a woman to wear pants and boots.

Cause: _____
Effect: Alice wore long skirts, high-top shoes, and bustles on hikes.

©Macmillan/McGraw-Hill

D. Alice continued to hike in the Rockies during the 1880s. At the time, much was known about eastern plants, but western plants were still largely unknown. Alice identified thousands of plants and became one of the world's experts on Rocky Mountain wildflowers. Even the famous British naturalist, Alfred Russel Wallace, paid a visit to Alice in 1887 to learn about these plants. Alice took Wallace on a hike, showing him many wildflowers that grew only in the Rockies.

Cause: _____

Effect: Alfred Russel Wallace paid a visit to Alice's classroom.

E. In 1890, Alice stopped teaching and devoted her life to her flower collection. Alice moved to San Francisco where she became curator at the California Academy of Sciences. From 1893 on, Alice's flower collection grew to be one of finest in the world. Then in 1906, San Francisco suffered a huge earthquake. Fires destroyed the academy and much of Alice's collection was lost.

Cause: An earthquake struck San Francisco in 1906.

Effect: _____

F. After the earthquake, Alice traveled to different parts of the world. Over the years, Alice's collection was restored and her fame spread far and wide. She wrote books on botany, and helped plan San Francisco's famous Golden Gate Park. Alice was even one of the first to notice how natural fires could help a plant community. Fires "cleansed" the community and allowed new types of seeds to grow. Today, thanks to Alice, many forest managers recognize the positive effects of natural fires.

Cause: _____

Effect: People learned that fires can be helpful to plant communities.

G. In 1950, Alice became the honorary president of the 7th International Botanical Congress in Sweden. She had become a world leader in botanical science. Her flower collection was immense, and her knowledge of western plants unmatched. In her honor, a plant was named after her—Eastwoodia elegans. In 1954, when Alice died, she was recognized as a pioneer in botany and one of the most remarkable women in science.

©Macmillan/McGraw-Hill

Cause: _____

Effect: Alice was elected honorary president of the congress.

Cross
Curricular
Activity 2

Tree Ring Dates

Connection to Social Studies and Math

Computation skills help you analyze the rings of a tree's trunk and match them to historical events.

Alice Eastwood saw giant redwood trees for the first time in 1890 when she visited California. Redwoods can live for hundreds, and even thousands, of years. The age of any tree can be measured by counting its tree rings.

Procedures

A. This drawing shows the rings in part of a trunk of a 500-year-old redwood tree. What historical events took place while this tree was growing? Use your social studies book or other reference books to identify the year each event listed below took place. Write the number of each event in its approximate location on the drawing.

1. The Declaration of Independence is signed.

2. World War II begins.

3. The Aztec and the Spanish meet for the first time.

4. The Jamestown Colony is founded.

5. Martin Luther King Jr. leads the March on Washington.

6. The Iroquois Confederacy forms.

7. The Pueblo Revolt occurs.

8. Triangular Trade grows in the colonies.

9. The Cold War ends.

10. Theodore Roosevelt is elected president.

11. Thomas Jefferson is elected president.

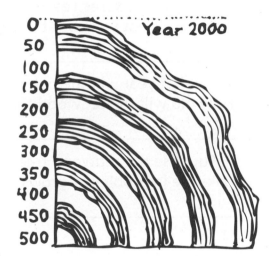

©Macmillan/McGraw-Hill

B. Solve each problem.

1. Alice Eastwood graduated from high school when the 500-year-old tree had 379 rings. In what year did Alice graduate from high school?

_____

2. The famous naturalist Alfred Russel Wallace visited Alice Eastwood when he was 64 years old. At that time, the redwood tree had 387 rings. During what year was Wallace born?

_____

3. A nearby oak tree has 423 more rings than the redwood tree. How old was the oak tree in the year 2000? When did it begin its life?

_____

4. The oak tree in problem 3 measures 271.6 feet in height. It is 47.8 feet taller than the redwood tree. How tall is the redwood tree?

_____

5. The redwood tree reached a height of 200 feet 56 years before its 400th birthday. What year was this? How old was the tree?

_____

6. In what year will the oak tree in problem 3 reach the age of 1,000 years? How old will the redwood tree be at that time?

_____

7. Suppose the redwood tree reaches a height of 300 feet in 100 years. If the oak tree in problem 4 grows the same amount, how tall will it be then?

_____

©Macmillan/McGraw-Hill

Plant Key

Connection to Language Arts
Using language precisely helps you identify organisms.

Alice Eastwood identified thousands of different plants during her lifetime. In most cases, she made the identifications without even using a picture. How did Alice tell her plants apart? She used a key. A key is a guide that uses language very precisely to identify a plant or other organism.

Procedures

Look at the drawing of the plants. Beginning at Step A, follow the directions in the key to help you identify the plants.

A. Does the plant have true roots?

- If yes, skip to B.
- If no, answer this question:

Are the leaflike parts liver-shaped or thin and fuzzy?

- If liver-shaped, the plant is a **liverwort**.
- If thin and fuzzy, the plant is a **moss**.

B. Does the plant have spores?

- If no, skip to C.
- If you can't tell, skip to C.
- If yes, answer this question:

Does the plant have broad, thin leaves?

- If broad, thin leaves, the plant is a **fern**.
- If no leaves, the plant is a **horsetail**.

C. Does the plant have flowers or cones?

- If flowers, skip to D.
- If cones, answer this question:

Does the plant lose its leaves in winter?

- If the leaves turn brown and fall off, the plant is a **larch**.
- If the leaves stay dark green and don't fall off, the plant is a **pine tree**.

D. Do the flower petals grow in groups of 3, or groups of 4 and 5?

- If groups of 4 or 5, the plant is a **dicot**. Skip to E.
- If groups of 3, the plant is a **monocot**. Answer this question:

Does the plant live in water or soil?

- If water, the plant is a **water lily**.
- If soil, the plant is an **iris**.

©Macmillan/McGraw-Hill

E. Does the plant have 4 or 5 petals?

- If 4 petals, skip to F.
- If 5 petals, answer this question:

Are the edges of each petal notched or rounded?

- If notched, the plant is a **rough-fruited cinquefoil**.
- If rounded, the plant is a **bulbous buttercup**.

F. Are there 6 or 8 stamens?

- If 6 stamens, the plant is a **field mustard**.
- If 8 stamens, the plant is an **evening primrose**.

PLANT 1

1. _____

PLANT 5

5. _____

PLANT 9

9. _____

PLANT 2

2. _____

SPORE
PLANT 6

6. _____

PLANT 10
CONE

10. _____

CONE
PLANT 3

3. _____

PLANT 7

7. _____

PLANT 11

11. _____

PLANT 4

4. _____

PLANT 8

8. _____

PLANT 12

12. _____

©Macmillan/McGraw-Hill

Animal Puzzle

Connection to Language Arts
Crossword puzzles help you use clues to identify the correct descriptive words

Alice Eastwood studied plants. Many naturalists study animals. Jane Goodall spent many years of her life studying chimpanzees in Africa.
You can study animals too. A fun way to sum up what you learn is to make a crossword puzzle based on animals. First try this one and then make up a puzzle of your own.

Across

3. Animals in the _____ group breathe through lungs. Most have waterproof scales.

6. Animals in the _____ group, for their size, have larger brains than other vertebrates.

8. Eagles are covered in feathers, but bats, cats, and mice are covered in _____.

9. Vertebrates are animals with backbones. Animals without backbones are called _____.

Down

1. Young mammals drink their mother's _____.

2. Some butterflies are hard to see because they blend into plants. Because of this adaptation called _____, many predators do not see the butterfly.

4. Frogs and toads belong to the _____ group of vertebrates.

5. Some harmless insects avoid predators because they resemble stinging insects. An adaptation called _____ gives the harmless insects a selective advantage.

7. Most fish are grouped together because they have gills and scales and because they _____.

8. A living thing with parents who are very different from each other is called a _____.

©Macmillan/McGraw-Hill

Now work with a group to make an animal crossword puzzle of your own.

1. Make a list of important animal words. Then try to connect the words across and down by finding letters the words have in common.

2. Draw a grid of boxes that matches the spacing of the words. Number the rows across and down.

3. Write a clue for each word. Hand the grid and the clues to another group to solve the puzzle.

©Macmillan/McGraw-Hill

A Butterfly Adaptation

Connection to Reading and Language Arts

Take notes while you read, and summarize your notes to help you understand the main ideas of what you read.

> Henry Walter Bates was another naturalist. He explored an adaptation called mimicry. As you read about his work, take notes of the most important ideas.

In 1862, Henry Walter Bates was studying butterflies in the rain forests of Brazil. He noticed that some kinds of butterflies were poisonous to birds. They were safe from these predators because birds stayed away from the poisonous butterflies. Birds fed on butterflies that were safe to eat.

After a while he noticed that some kinds of butterflies that were not poisonous had evolved to look like the poisonous kinds of butterflies. In time, he understood that their similar warning marks helped to protect them from their predators and increased their chances of surviving.

These markings were an example of mimicry. Mimicry is an adaptation different from camouflage. Camouflaged animals blend and "become lost" in their environment. Mimicry enables some species to mimic, or imitate, other, more dangerous, animals.

Summarize what you just read.

_____

_____

_____

_____

© Macmillan/McGraw-Hill

Plant Journal

Connection to Language Arts and Art

Language arts and art skills help you learn more about the natural world around you.

> Alice Eastwood identified thousands of plants during her lifetime. To tell her plants apart, Alice kept a plant journal. You can keep your own plant journal, too.

Procedures

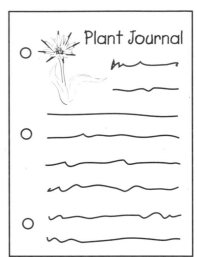

1. You'll need materials that include a sketchbook and colored pencils or pens. If possible, use a magnifying lens to get a good look at each plant you find.

2. Bring your journal equipment with you whenever you go out walking. Draw each new plant you find. Be sure to include as many details as possible in your drawing. Use your magnifying lens to get a close look at the plant. Try to record the number of petals, type of leaves, and the type of seeds.

3. Make a note of the date, the time, where you found the plant, when it blooms, and any other information you think is important. Photograph the plant and its environment if you have a camera.

4. Record any questions, thoughts, observations, and opinions you may have. Refer back to them as you learn more about the plants you found.

5. Use a key or field guide book to identify each plant. Record the plant's scientific name in your journal.

6. Return to the locations of the plants you have identified during different times of the year. Make a note of how each plant changes and what it looks like.

7. What do you find enjoyable about keeping a plant journal? What new and interesting things did you learn?

©Macmillan/McGraw-Hill

Model Ecosystem

Connection to Art and Language Arts

Building and labeling a model is an effective way to communicate science concepts.

The **Nature Network** is a television network devoted to creating educational programs about nature. One of the network's first programs will be about ecosystems. Remember, the living and nonliving things in an environment and all their interactions make up an ecosystem.

The producers are trying to decide which types of ecosystems to highlight in the program. Your class is the group of science specialists that they have hired as consultants. Your assignment is to create, label, and describe a model of an ecosystem you think would be a good choice for this program.

Procedures

1. Work with your group to choose an ecosystem that you would like to model. Look out a window. What types of ecosystems do you see? Remember, an ecosystem can be as small as a puddle of water or as large as a forest.

2. As you design and build you model, think about what the living things need to survive. Carefully label all the different parts of your model. Write a brief description of all the parts of your model and how they all interact. Try to use as many of the following science words as possible:

   - abiotic factors
   - adaptations
   - biotic factors
   - community
   - consumers
   - decomposer
   - ecosystem
   - habitat
   - niche
   - population
   - producer

3. Each group should take turns presenting its model to the class. As a class, decide which ecosystems should be included in the program. What factors did you use to evaluate the models and make your choices?

©Macmillan/McGraw-Hill

Niche Battles

Connection to Language Arts
Language arts skills help you effectively communicate science concepts.

The **Nature Network** has a new series called "Niche Battles." The series investigates what happens when the niches of two organisms conflict with each other. The producers have asked you to prepare background information for our new programs in the series.

Write a paragraph explaining your prediction of what will happen in each situation.

1. At one time, the arrival of the Cuban anoles in Florida caused the green anoles to find a new niche. Suppose another new anole is introduced in Florida. They are faster than the large Cuban anoles and better hunters. The Cuban anoles are so large and heavy that they can't live in the small branches in the treetops. How do you think each anole's population and niche will change?

2. Normal rye grass for lawns is invaded by crabgrass. Crabgrass is faster-growing, needs less water, and is more resistant to disease than rye grass. How do you think each grass's population and niche will change?

3. Owls move into a niche occupied by hawks. They both hunt field mice and other small prey. The owls hunt at night only. How do you think each bird's population and niche will change?

4. Large trees begin to grow in a field where shrubs and tall grasses grow. These trees begin to block the sunlight that the grasses and shrubs need. How do you think each plant's population and niche will change?

©Macmillan/McGraw-Hill

Predators and Prey

Connection to Math

Understanding probability can help you see relationships between predators and prey.

> The **Nature Network's** new hit game show is called "Predators and Prey." This game helps you visualize the outcomes of different types of predator-prey relationships. Follow these directions on how to make and play your own home version of the game.

Getting Started

1. Decide which player will represent predators and which player will represent prey.

2. Make a spinner as shown. Shade $\frac{1}{2}$ of the sections one color to represent predators. Shade the other $\frac{1}{2}$ of the sections another color to represent prey. Use a straightened paper clip with a bent tip as a pointer. Insert the bent tip into the center of the spinner.

3. "Predators" should make 10 cards. Use paper that is the same color as the shaded sections on the spinner representing predators. "Prey" should make 30 cards. Use paper that is the same color as the shaded sections on the spinner representing prey.

©Macmillan/McGraw-Hill

To Play

1. Predators should start with 3 cards. Prey should start with 12 cards. Place the other cards in two piles on the table in front of you.

2. Each player should takes turns spinning the spinner. If the pointer lands on a predator section, the predator wins. Remove one card from the prey's deck and place it back on the pile. If the pointer lands on a prey section, add one prey card to the player's cards.

3. If the predator loses 3 times in a row, remove one predator card from the predator's deck. If the predator wins 3 times in a row, add one predator card to the predator's deck.

4. Keep playing until one player loses all of his or her cards. Record your results.

Analyze the Game

1. What was probability that the predators would win any one spin in the game? Prey?

2. Was the probability of predators winning the game higher, lower, or equal to the probability of prey winning? Who actually won the game? Why?

3. What do the results of the game tell you about a predator-prey relationship where each animal has an equal chance for survival?

4. What do you think will happen if predators in an area have a much greater chance for survival and eat most of the prey?

©Macmillan/McGraw-Hill

Biome Map

Connection to Social Studies
Map reading skills can help you locate Earth's major biomes.

The **Nature Network** is airing a special called "Biomes of the World" that explores Earth's major biomes. The network published a map to help its viewers prepare for the program. Use the map and its key to test your map-reading skills and knowledge of geography. Will you be ready for the program?

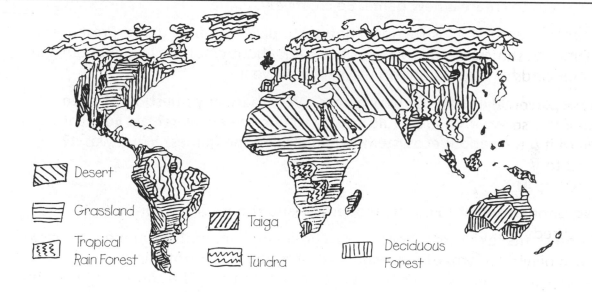

Desert

Grassland

Tropical
Rain Forest

Taiga

Tundra

Deciduous
Forest

1. Which continents have tundra? _____

2. Which continents would you visit to see a tropical rain forest?

_____

3. Which continent has the smallest area of tropical rain forest?

_____

4. Which continent has the largest grassland? What kind of grassland is it?

_____

5. Which continents have the greatest number of different biomes?

_____

6. Which continent has the largest desert? _____

© Macmillan/McGraw-Hill

Cross Curricular
Culminating Activity

Design a Game

Connection to Language Arts
Language arts skills help you effectively communicate science concepts.

> The **Nature Network** would like to produce a new game show. The producers are inviting viewers to design and submit ideas for new games. A contest will be held to choose the most interesting and exciting game.

1. Play the Eco-Challenge game described below. After playing the game, use it for ideas to create a new game. Be creative!

2. Carefully write the instructions for how to play your new game. Present the game to your classmates. Ask for feedback about what they liked about the game and for suggestions on ways to improve it.

3. Take turns playing all the new games. Were there any questions that you couldn't answer? Where could you go to find the answers? Did you learn anything new about ecosystems while playing the games? What was it?

Eco-Challenge

1. Name one student to be the moderator and choose three contestants.

2. Contestants take turns choosing categories and amounts of money. All answers must be in the form of a question. A contestant plays until he or she gives an incorrect answer. Then it's the next contestant's turn. The contestant with the most money at the end of the game wins.

The Blackland Prairie	Producers, Consumers, & Decomposers	Parts of an Ecosystem	You Are What You Eat
$400 Important activity of the eastern spadefoot toad	**$400** Gas that producers give off and consumers need	**$400** Nonliving part of an ecosystem	**$400** Organism that eats all types of food
$300 How the Blackland Prairie got its name	**$300** Gas that consumers give off and producers need	**$300** Living part of an ecosystem	**$300** Organism that only eats plants
$200 Large hoofed animal that roams the area	**$200** What decomposers do	**$200** Group of organisms that are all the same	**$200** Organism that only eats other animals
$100 Most common plant in Blacklands	**$100** What producers make	**$100** Place where a population lives	**$100** What a predator hunts

©Macmillan/McGraw-Hill

Hank Hudson, Geo-Explorer

Connection to Math

Computation skills can help you find the distance each planet travels in one orbit of the Sun.

> Meet Hank Hudson, a **Geo-Explorer**. Geo-Explorers explore the world and beyond looking for adventure and to learn more about science. Hank's new adventure is investigating how far each planet travels in one orbit of the Sun.

You can help Hank make his computations. First use the table to find a planet's distance from the Sun. Then multiply that distance by 6.3 to find the approximate distance the planet travels in one orbit of the Sun.

1. How far is Mercury from the Sun? Approximately how many millions of miles does Mercury travel in one orbit of the Sun? _____

2. Calculate the distance each planet travels in one orbit of the Sun.

_____
_____
_____
_____
_____
_____
_____
_____
_____
_____

PLANET	MILLIONS OF MILES FROM THE SUN
Mercury	36
Venus	67
Earth	93
Mars	142
Jupiter	483
Saturn	886
Uranus	1,783
Neptune	2,793
Pluto	3,666

©Macmillan/McGraw-Hill

3. Which planet travels the shortest distance in one orbit? The farthest distance?

_____

4. How much farther does Mars travel in one orbit than Earth?

_____

5. Which travels farther in one orbit, Earth or Mercury? How much farther?

_____

6. Which travels farther in one orbit, Venus or Saturn? How much farther?

_____

7. How many millions of miles does Earth travel in two orbits around the Sun?

_____

8. Which is farther: one orbit of Mars or two orbits of Earth? How much farther?

_____

9. Which is farther: one orbit of Jupiter or 5 orbits of Earth? How much farther?

_____

10. Which is farther: one orbit of Pluto or 4 orbits of Saturn? How much farther?

_____

©Macmillan/McGraw-Hill

Earthquake Map

Connection to Social Studies

Map skills can help you locate places where earthquakes typically occur.

The **Geo-Explorers** are planning a trip to visit the earthquake zones of the world. Before they can go, they need to make a map of where earthquakes occur. They have asked you to help them plan their trip.

Use these clues to locate the world's earthquake zones on the map provided on the next page. Use a reference map if necessary. Draw in each earthquake zone on the map.

1. A band of earthquakes runs from the Aleutian Islands off Alaska along the west coast of North America. The zone extends all the way to the edge of South America.

2. An earthquake band runs from the western edge of Cuba across the West Indies, through Venezuela to the west coast of South America. It extends all the way to the tip of the continent.

3. An earthquake band runs from Greece to Turkey to Iran, all the way to the India-China border. Then, it turns south through Malaysia and follows the East Indies all the way to New Zealand.

4. The band that begins at the Aleutians (question 1) goes east through Japan and the Philippines and joins up with the band described in Step 3 near Papua/New Guinea.

©Macmillan/McGraw-Hill

©Macmillan/McGraw-Hill

Hank's Tricky Mysteries

Connection to Reading

Paying careful attention to details whenreading can provide clues to help answer a question.

> The **Geo-Explorers** come across plenty of mysteries on their adventures. All Geo-Explorers record their adventures in journals. Hank has recorded five "mysteries" in his journal. He planned to solve them when he returned home from his latest adventure. Can you help him? Pay attention to the main idea, supporting details, and the sequence of events in each journal entry.

1. **Friday, March 5th** We are looking to find a place that has crocodile fossils. We found three likely spots, each with sedimentary rock. Location 1 has coquina rock. Location 2 has bituminous coal. Location 3 has sandstone. In which location should we look?

2. **Wednesday, March 17th** On a rock hunt, we found four "mystery minerals" which we called A, B, C, and D. Mineral B was scratched by C. Mineral D was able to scratch C. Mineral A was scratched by B. How do the minerals rank in order of their hardness?

3. **Thursday, March 25th** On the site of a fossil dig, our off-road vehicle got a big greenish-black scratch on its fender. We were so tired that we have forgotten where the site was. We searched far and wide for it, but all we could find was a place with a big yellow pyrite rock, not a green rock. What could have happened?

4. **Monday, April 5th** Two workers are arguing over where some very large quartz crystals were found. Lainee says the crystals came from deep underground. Dan says the crystals were just sitting on the ground. Which worker is more likely to be right?

5. **Tuesday, April 13th** Two farmers share a hill. Each plowed one side of the hill. The farmer on the west side saw all of his soil erode away. The east side farmer's soil did not erode. Why did one side of the hill have so much more erosion than the other?

©Macmillan/McGraw-Hill

Water Waste

Connection to Math
Computation skills can help you identify how much water is wasted by a leaky faucet.

> The **Geo-Explorers** want to stop water waste—now! One way to help people understand how much water is wasted is to provide an example, like a leaky faucet. How much water do you think a leaky faucet wastes in one year? You might be surprised!

Procedures

1. Find a faucet that leaks or create an artificial leak by allowing water to drip slowly from a faucet.

2. Collect water in a container provided by your teacher for 15 minutes. Record the amount of water you collected.

Results

1. How much water leaked in the period of time that you measured? At this rate, how much water would leak in one hour?

   _____

2. How much water would leak in one whole day? How did you arrive at this number? _____

3. How much water would leak in one week? How did you arrive at this number? _____

4. How much water would leak in one month? How did you arrive at this number? _____

5. How much water would leak in one year? How did you arrive at this number? _____

6. How would you use this data to convince someone to fix a leaky faucet?

   _____

©Macmillan/McGraw-Hill

Energy Graphs

Connection to Math and Social Studies

Graphing skills can help you interpret information about energy use around the world.

Recently a group of **Geo-Explorers** investigated energy use around the world. They collected information about who uses energy and how it is used. These graphs show their findings.

Energy: Who Uses It? **Energy: What Do We Use It For?**

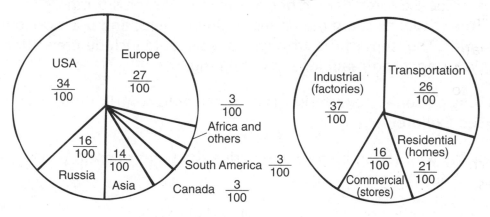

Use the graphs to answer these questions.

1. Which country or region uses the most energy? _____

2. Which continent uses the most energy? _____

3. Does the United States use more energy than France? How do you know?

   _____

4. Which two regions together use more than half of the world's energy?

   _____

5. Which countries or regions seem to be using their fair share of the world's energy resources? Which are using more than their fair share? Which are using less? _____

6. Which two energy uses together account for almost three-quarters of total energy use? _____

© Macmillan/McGraw-Hill

Cross Curricular
Culminating Activity

Be a Geo-Explorer Contest

Connection to Language Arts
Language arts and art skills help you write persuasive letters.

> How would you like to be a **Geo-Explorer**? Here's your chance to win a spot on the new Geo-Explorer team that is being organized. Follow these directions to enter the contest. You just might be chosen to join the team.

Procedures

1. Write a persuasive letter to the selection committee explaining why you would like to be a Geo-Explorer. Remember, a persuasive letter is composed to convince the reader to share the writer's opinion, facts, and practical ideas to argue a point. The steps of the writing process should include prewriting, drafting, revising, proofreading, and publishing.

2. Describe any personal characteristics you feel would contribute to making you a good Geo-Explorer.

3. When writing your letter, be sure to describe the types of areas you would like to explore. Your choices include:

   - Earth and it neighbors
   - Earth's crust and minerals
   - Rocks and soil
   - Earth's atmosphere
   - Earth's water supply
   - Energy resources

4. Explain what you already know about the areas you chose. Also describe the types of topics you would like to investigate to learn more about them.

5. Form several "selection committees" to evaluate the contest letters. Compare the letters to identify the types of features that persuaded the selection committees to choose Geo-Explorer candidates. Share those features as a class.

6. Would you like to make any changes to your letter based on these findings? Why or why not? If so, what types of changes would you make?

©Macmillan/McGraw - Hill

Storm of the Century

Connection to Reading and Language Arts

Reading and writing skills help you understand the effects of weather and a natural disaster.

> Galveston, Texas is located in the Gulf of Mexico. Galveston had always been a prime target for hurricanes. For the most part, people seemed to take storms in stride. Then, in 1900, a hurricane struck that no one would ever forget. Killing between 6,000 and 8,000 people, the storm has been called the worst recorded natural disaster ever to strike the North American continent.

Procedures

Read the story of the Galveston hurricane below and write a summary sentence for each paragraph.

1. On Friday, September 7, 1900, the people of Galveston sat down to supper. It was a windy night, but few of the residents felt any cause for alarm. At that time, Galveston was a bustling seaport, the fourth largest city in Texas. In 1900, Galveston had a population of 37,789. The only link between the island and the mainland was a three-mile long wagon bridge and three railroad trestles. By the following evening, the entire island would be leveled by a devastating hurricane. Some 8,000 people would be killed by what has been called the "greatest natural disaster of the 20th century" in the United States.

2. Galveston is an island with a tropical climate that is located two miles off the Texas coast. People were used to storms on Galveston. The last big storm had struck in 1876 and few people had been killed. However, Galveston stood only 8.7 feet above sea level at its highest point. This caused many people to worry about what would happen if a truly big storm were to strike.

3. Among those who worried about storms was Dr. Isaac Cline. Dr. Cline was Galveston's weather bureau chief. In those days, sophisticated electronic equipment that measured air pressure, water vapor, and air movement were unheard of. There was no way to quickly transmit data that was collected. Most reliable weather information traveled by telegraph or by ship. On September 6, Dr. Cline got word that a hurricane-force storm was heading toward Galveston. Dr. Cline tried to warn the residents of the approaching storm. Unfortunately, few people took his warning seriously enough to leave the island.

©Macmillan/McGraw-Hill

4. A strong wind from the north arrived on Friday evening. For a while, it fought off the hurricane, which approached from the south. On Saturday morning, spectators lined the beaches to view the huge waves in Galveston Bay. Little did they know that they would soon be trapped. They were cut off from the mainland as the island's bridges were destroyed.

5. By late Saturday, the barometer reading on the island reached a low of 28.44 inches. Meanwhile, the wind speed continued to increase. The anemometer showed a final reading of 102 miles per hour before it was swept away. Before long, the winds would reach speeds of over 120 mph, demolishing nearly everything in their path. The city's gasworks were destroyed, plunging the island into total darkness. Brick buildings caved in like paper cups. Roofs were torn off of buildings. Deadly debris flew in every direction. Soon, rising waters put the entire island underwater.

6. To escape the destruction, people did what they could. Many of those who were saved went to the Tremont Hotel. Others weren't so lucky. They tried to escape in boats. Others fled to their rooftops. Still others were carried away in the water, holding onto scraps of wood or tree limbs. The full force of the hurricane struck at about 4 o'clock on Saturday. By midnight the storm was gone.

7. Wreckage from the storm was beyond belief. On Sunday, survivors surveyed the damage. Destruction was almost total. Not a single building on the island was without damage. Most of the buildings were flattened, but the island's residents didn't give up. Following the disaster they worked hard to rebuild the city. This included a massive sea wall to protect the island. For the most part, it has protected Galveston from the kind of destruction that took place on September 8, 1900.

©Macmillan/McGraw-Hill

Cross
Curricular
Activity 2

Tracking the Storm

Connection to Social Studies

Social studies skills help you understand the path of the 1900 Galveston storm.

Procedures

1. Use the information provided to track the path of the storm on a wall map. Nine volunteers should each write the letter for a step listed below on a small piece of paper with a sticky edge. Also include the date the storm was spotted. Be sure the paper can be removed without damaging the map.

2. Have volunteers take turns placing the papers on the map. Work as a class to find the exact place each should go.

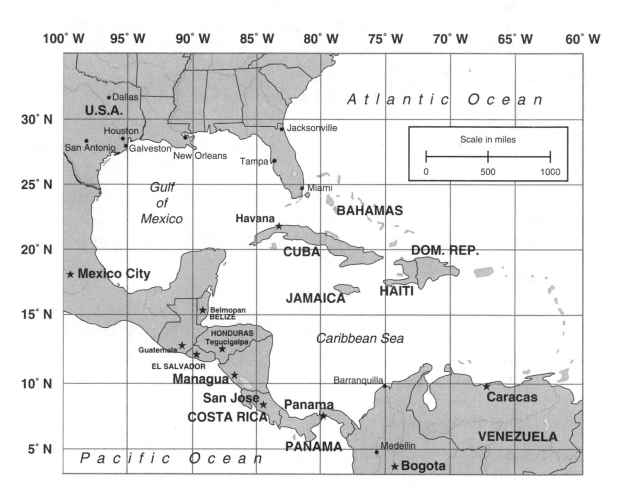

© Macmillan/McGraw-Hill

a. The storm was first sighted on August 30th, 1900 near the Windward Islands at 15° N and 63° W.

b. On the morning of August 31st the storm was still at 15° N but had moved to longitude 67° W about 200 miles south of Puerto Rico.

c. On September 1st, the storm was located 200 miles south of Santo Domingo in the Dominican Republic.

d. On September 2nd, the storm was located only a few miles southwest of the island of Jamaica.

e. On September 3rd, the storm was located at 21° N and 81° W, about 175 miles south of the center portion of the island of Cuba. On that day, 12.58 inches of rain fell on the city of Santiago, Cuba.

f. The storm center passed over the center of Cuba on September 4th. High winds were reported but the storm was still not at full strength.

g. On September 5th and 6th, the storm moved northward toward Key West, at the southern tip of Florida. At this point it was unclear whether the storm would move up the east or west coastline of the Florida peninsula.

h. On September 7th, the storm hugged the gulf coastline, south of central Louisiana. At this point, the city of Galveston was given an official warning. Few people left the island. Most had been through storms before and saw nothing to worry about.

i. On the morning of September 8th, the storm was reported to be at 28° N and 94° W. This was just before Galveston was hit. At this point, barometric pressure on Galveston was at 29.22 inches with a northeast wind of 42 miles per hour.

3. Form small groups. Each group should take turns approaching the map to solve the following problems using the information on the labels and the map's scale. Estimate your answers.

a. On September 3rd, how far was the storm from Galveston? _____

b. How many miles did the storm move between September 6th and the morning of September 8th? _____

c. About how many miles did the storm move from August 31st to September 8th?

_____

©Macmillan/McGraw-Hill

Name_____ Date_____

Cross Curricular
Activity 3

Comparing Hurricanes

Connection to Math
Using a table and a bar graph can help you compare different hurricanes.

> Hurricanes differ in how powerful they are. They are rated in categories from 1 to 5. A category 1 hurricane is less powerful than a category 5 hurricane. The table shows wind speeds and heights of storm waves for the different categories. The bar graph compares four 1998 hurricanes to the Galveston hurricane of 1900.

Category	Winds (mph)	Storm Wave
1	74–95	4–5 ft
2	96–100	6–8 ft
3	111–130	9–12 ft
4	131–155	13–18 ft
5	155+	18+ ft

Hurricane Wind Speeds

Mitch 1998
Bonnie 1998
Earl 1998
Georges 1998
Galveston 1900

0   50   100   150   200
Wind Speed in mph

Use the table and the bar graph to solve the problems.

1. Which hurricane was a category 4 hurricane? _____

   What size storm wave would you expect it to have had? _____

2. What was the most powerful hurricane in the group? _____

   How does it compare to the Galveston hurricane? _____

3. The Galveston hurricane had a storm wave of 15.7 feet. How much larger was this wave than the largest wave for a category 3 hurricane? _____

4. Which hurricane would you have expected to do the least amount of damage?

   What category was this hurricane? _____

5. Suppose a hurricane had wind speeds that were halfway between the speeds of Georges and Mitch. How fast would its winds be? _____

©Macmillan/McGraw-Hill

Cross Curricular
Activity 4

Survivor Stories

Connection to Reading
Science helps you infer the meanings of words and situations.

> Experiencing a hurricane of any category is a terrifying, and often deadly, experience. These survivor stories give you an idea of what it was like to experience the Galveston hurricane.

Use context clues to infer about the words and events in each story.

The Boss Family's Story Mrs. Boss, formerly of Chicago, was seated at supper with her son and husband when the storm broke. They escaped to the second story of their house. When the powerful water reached them, they <u>hurtled</u> into the darkness and landed on a wooden cistern. Several times Mrs. Boss lost her hold of the <u>cistern</u> and fell into the water, only to be pulled up again by her son. After the storm they were finally found. Mrs. Boss' feet were crushed and bleeding and her clothing was torn. The men's clothing had been torn from their bodies. The Boss family were the only persons from the entire block to survive. How ironic that an object holding water saved them from drowning.

Infer: What does the word *hurtled* mean?

_____

Infer: What is a *cistern* and how did it help save the Boss family?

_____

Mr. Fewell's Story After the storm, C. H. Fewell wrote, "I got up about 4 o'clock Saturday. It was raining and blowing hard. I left the house, ran for the Tremont Hotel and came near not making it. We stayed there all night. Every passing minute I thought that the building would certainly go with the many that were going to pieces around it." Luckily, Mr. Fewell survived the storm <u>unscathed</u>.

Infer: What does the word *unscathed* mean?

_____

Infer: How did Mr. Fewell feel during the storm?

_____

©Macmillan/McGraw-Hill

The Irwin Family's Story During the storm, Mr. and Mrs. James Irwin floated off on separate sections of the roof of their house. Eventually Mr. Irwin found <u>refuge</u> at the Ursuline Convent. On the next day, he thought he would never see his wife again. Then he heard a cry for help. Hoping to rescue someone, Mr. Irwin was surprised and overjoyed to find his wife still afloat on a part of the roof.

Infer: What does the word *refuge* mean?

_____

Infer: Where had Mrs. Irwin been all night?

_____

Mr. Frost's Story Early Sunday morning Jack Frost walked into the Tremont Hotel and fainted. Frost was bruised from head to foot. The doctors said that the bones of his right hand were broken. His left shoulder joint was <u>dislocated</u> and horribly bruised and mangled. He had been caught at Murdock's pavilion on the beach when the storm came up, and could not get away. No one knew where he landed at the end of the storm.

Infer: What does the word *dislocated* mean?

_____

Infer: What happened to Jack Frost?

_____

Mr. Lundwall's Story Emil C. Lundwall was aboard a large ship anchored between jetties in the harbor with a 1,500-pound anchor. The pounding of the large waves broke the boat's <u>moorings</u>. It traveled a distance of about four miles to a point where it was <u>grounded.</u> Although it is not easy to get a grounded boat back into the water, there wasn't much damage to the boat— mainly broken windows. Lundwall was a skillful seaman who used his knowledge of navigating a boat to save his vessel.

Infer: What are *moorings*?

_____

Infer: What happens when a boat is *grounded?*

_____

©Macmillan/McGraw - Hill

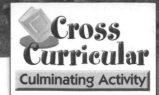

Hurricane Report

Connection to Language Arts, Social Studies, and Art

Language arts, social studies, and art skills can help you learn more about hurricanes and create an illustrated report.

> Hurricane season typically begins in late summer and lasts until mid-fall. During hurricane season you can track hurricanes in the news media as they occur. Otherwise, you can use books, magazines, and the Internet to find out about a hurricane of the past. Use the information you collect to create an illustrated hurricane report.

Procedures

1. **Get Started** If it is hurricane season, find out about current hurricanes using the following resources: newspapers, news magazines, and the Internet. Useful web sites include: the National Hurricane Center, Federal Emergency Management Agency (FEMA), and www.disasterrelief.org. To learn about past hurricanes on the Internet, click on a "hurricane history" button, or use a search engine to look up individual hurricanes by name.

2. **Collect Information** Use your resources to collect information about the storm. How and when did the storm form? What was its path? How much damage did it do? What was its wind speed and storm wave height?

3. **Communicate** Many hurricane web sites include stories from survivors. Collect some of the survivors' stories if they are available.

4. **Assemble** Write a report that tells the story of the hurricane. Be sure to include as many of the following features as possible: tracking maps, weather maps, charts, graphs, data, survivor stories, news accounts, photographs, and damage reports. Your report should include an introduction, a body, and a conclusion.

5. **Present** Present your report to the class. You may give a live presentation, or display your report on a bulletin board. Form groups to compare and contrast the hurricanes that you reported on.

© Macmillan/McGraw-Hill

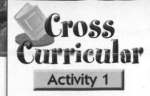

Bowling in Space

Connection to Math
Multiplication and ordering decimals can help you compare weights of objects on different planets and on the Moon.

Welcome to **Matter Magazine**—The Magazine that matters. At *Matter Magazine*, we have articles about *anything*—as long as it is about things made of matter.

The new issue of *Matter Magazine* features an article about the possibility of bowling in space as a sport of the future. Suppose bowling on the Moon, and on other planets, was possible. It would be different from bowling on Earth in one important way. The effects of gravity vary on the Moon and other planets. For example, things weigh only 0.167, or about $\frac{1}{6}$, as much on the Moon as they do on Earth. How would the weight of a bowler and her equipment be affected by gravity in different places?

1. Multiply to find the weights of the objects in the chart on the next page. Remember, multiplying decimals is like multiplying money amounts. Be sure to insert the decimal point when you are done. You may use a calculator to check your answers once you complete the chart.

2. Use the data from the chart to compare and order, from least to greatest, the weights of objects in different places. You may use a number line to help you if you wish. Where do objects weigh the most? The least?

_____

_____

_____

©Macmillan/McGraw-Hill

Comparing Weights			
Color	**120-newton bowling ball**	**20-newton bowling pin**	**470-newton person**
Earth Multiply by 1.0	120 newtons	20 newtons	470 newtons
Moon Multiply by 0.167			
Mars Multiply by 0.38			
Jupiter Multiply by 2.64			
Saturn Multiply by 1.16			

Units of Weight (metric/customary)

1 newton (N) = 0.22 pound (lb)

1 pound = 4.45 newtons

© Macmillan/McGraw - Hill

Dmitry Mendeleyev

Connection to Reading

Reading skills help you learn about the people who contributed to advances in science.

> *Matter Magazine* recently published a short article on the chemist Dmitry Mendeleyev. Read the article, then answer the questions.

All matter is made of elements. An important tool used to study matter and the elements is the periodic table. However, this useful tool didn't always exist. Who created it and when? The answer is Dmitry Mendeleyev in 1869. Mendeleyev was a Russian chemist who lived from 1834 to 1907.

About 63 elements were known to chemists by 1860. From studying the elements, many chemists realized that the elements could be classified into groups based on similar chemical properties. Mendeleyev observed that elements with similar properties were periodic, repeating in a certain pattern. He arranged the elements in a chart according to their mass. This was a very good idea, but there were some problems. Other scientists then arranged the elements according to their atomic number, or the number of protons in an atom of a specific element. This is the basis of the periodic table of the elements used today.

1. **Main Idea** What is the main idea of this article?

2. **Context Clues** Use context clues to help you determine the meaning of the words *periodic* and *atomic number*.

3. **Make Inferences** Why do you think the periodic table of the elements was given its name?

4. **Summarize** How would you summarize this passage?

©Macmillan/McGraw-Hill

Water Graphs

Connection to Math
Graphs help you compare data.

People who live on high mountains claim that the boiling point of water is lower than at sea level. *Matter Magazine* ran tests to see if the boiling point of water is lower at high altitudes. Ice was placed in two containers. One container was tested at sea level and the other was tested at a high altitude. The same amount of heat was applied to each container until the water in each boiled. These graphs show the results of the tests.

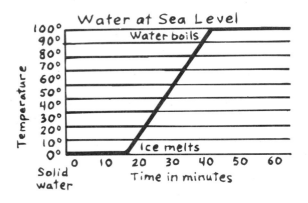

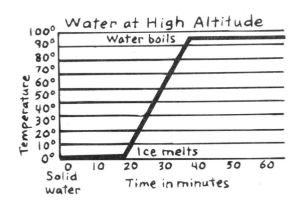

Use the data from the graphs to answer the questions.

1. How long does it take water to melt from a solid to a liquid at sea level? At a high altitude?

   _____

2. At approximately what time would you expect to find both ice and liquid water in the sea level container?

   _____

3. At approximately what time would you expect the sea level container to contain only liquid water?

   _____

©Macmillan/McGraw-Hill

4. At approximately what time would you expect to find both liquid water and water vapor in the high altitude container?

_____

5. At what temperature does liquid water change to water vapor at sea level? At a high altitude?

_____

6. What is the boiling point of water at sea level? At a high altitude?

_____

7. How does the boiling point of water at high altitude compare with the boiling point of water at sea level?

_____

8. Air pressure is less at higher altitudes than at sea level. How could the air pressure in each place affect the boiling point of water? Explain.

_____

_____

9. Predict the boiling point of water at 50,000 feet—higher than any mountain.

_____

10. At sea level, water's boiling point changes slightly from day to day. What might cause this change?

_____

_____

© Macmillan/McGraw-Hill

What's the Ingredient?

Connection to Health

Different types of foods can be described in terms of mixtures and compounds.

Each year, *Matter Magazine* prints a food issue that analyzes the ingredients of popular fast foods. In this issue, the magazine's writers wanted to use their knowledge of mixtures and compounds to describe each food. Unfortunately, they have lost their final notes. Can you describe each food based on their observations?

Magazine $2.50
Special Food Issue

Read the description of each food. Then decide if each is a mixture or a compound. If a food is a mixture, determine if it is a solution, a suspension, or a colloid. Explain.

1. **Cool River Drink** This clear, green liquid does not separate using filters. It does not settle into layers. It does not scatter light. When the liquid evaporates it leaves a green powder.

   _____

2. **Super Sauce** This thick sauce is dark, rich, and cloudy. When filtered, it leaves a dark solid on the filter paper. When allowed to settle, three layers form.

   _____

3. **Sweet Crystals** These white crystals cannot be separated using filters, evaporation, or settling. Under special conditions, the crystals change color, give off heat, and turn into two new substances. The new substances have a different color, taste, and texture than the original crystals.

   _____

4. **Swell Gel** This gel is partly clear, but it scatters light. It does not settle out into layers.

   _____

©Macmillan/McGraw-Hill

Cross Curricular
Culminating Activity

Invention Contest

Connection to Language Arts and Art
Language arts and art skills help you communicate science ideas clearly and effectively.

Have you ever wanted to invent something?
Enter the **Matter Magazine** Invention Contest!
Just follow the directions below.

Procedures

1. **Read** Almost everything you use today was invented by someone. How do you think people get ideas for their inventions? Read about some inventors like the people listed below, or anyone else you choose.

Invention	Year Invented	Inventor
Paper	1st century A.D.	Tsai Lun
Lightning Rod	1752	Benjamin Franklin
Sewing Machine	1830	Barthelemey Thimonnier
Steam Shovel	1838	William S. Otis
Safety Pin	1849	Walter Hunt
Typewriter	1868	Christopher Sholes, Carlos Glidden, Samuel Soulé
Telephone	1876	Alexander Graham Bell
Zipper	1896	W. L. Judson
Radio	1896	Guglielmo Marconi
Electric Razor	1923	Jacob Schick
Helicopter	1939	Igor Sikorsky

© Macmillan/McGraw - Hill

Cross
Curricular
Culminating Act. p.2

2. **Brainstorm** Inventions often come when people try to solve a problem or have a certain need. Work with your group to think of an idea for an invention. List your ideas to help you organize your thoughts. Try to make your invention as realistic as possible, but be imaginative!

3. **Write** Answer the following questions.

   a. What problem does your invention solve?

   _____

   b. Describe your invention and how it works.

   _____

   _____

   c. What kind of matter is your invention made of?

   _____

   d. How do the forms of matter help your invention work?

   _____

   _____

4. **Draw** On a separate sheet of paper draw a picture of your invention. Show and label its parts.

5. **Improve** Inventions take time to perfect. Input from others is very valuable. Take turns presenting your invention to your classmates. Does anyone have suggestions for improving it? Does anyone have any criticisms? How can each help improve your invention?

©Macmillan/McGraw-Hill

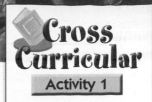

Celebrations Around the World

Connection to Reading

Reading skills help you compare how sound and light are used to celebrate events in different cultures.

> People all over the world enjoy celebrations. A celebration is a ritual or ceremony that marks an event such as an anniversary of some sort, the beginning or end of a season, or the passage of time. Many festive celebrations include special dances, processions, sounds, lights, and colors.

Read the following passages. Pay attention to the main idea and supporting details of each. Then, create a compare and contrast table. Use it to help you write a brief paragraph that compares and contrasts two holidays of your choice. Discuss the movements, sounds, and lights used, if possible.

Tet—Vietnamese New Year This seven-day festival celebrates the beginning of the new year and spring. Families clean their homes in preparation for the good things that will happen in the new year. They repay old debts. A tree made of bamboo decorated with red paper stands in each home to safeguard against evil spirits. Candles representing the Sun and Moon, and incense representing the stars, are burned. *Cau doi*, poems about the importance of the family, are written on red strips of paper and hung in the home. Parents often give children red envelopes with money. Sometimes there are noisy parades with a dragon leading the way.

Chinese New Year Near the end of each year some people believe the Chinese kitchen god journeys to the Emperor of Heaven. He reports on the families' thoughts and behaviors over the year. Families spread honey or sweets on the picture of the god so he will say sweet things about them. Then the picture is burned to allow the kitchen god to go on his journey. Families prepare for the five-day celebration by settling arguments, cleaning their homes, putting up decorations, and preparing food for visitors. The kitchen god is welcomed back on the eve of the New Year with a feast and fireworks. On New Year's Day families exchange gifts. A "money tree" is decorated with old coins and paper flowers. Parents give their children money wrapped in red paper for good luck. Parades led by enormous paper dragons or lions dance through the streets. Fireworks, beating drums, and shouting people help scare away the evil spirits that bring bad luck. This helps pave the way for good luck in the new year.

© Macmillan/McGraw-Hill

Diwali The Indian new year, Diwali, is celebrated with a five-day festival of light. Hindu families clean their homes. People sing, dance, and display fireworks. Flowers and bright colors are everywhere. Each night, lighted candle pots are placed on paths, tops of houses, and in windows. The lights welcome the goddess of prosperity, Lakshami, who may ensure good fortune and bring presents. The main theme of Diwali is that of goodness triumphing over evil and light over darkness. People celebrate the new year looking forward to a bright future.

Hanukkah or Chanukah The Jewish Festival of Lights dates back to 165 B.C., when the Syrians were defeated by the Jews after a three-year struggle. The Jews reclaimed their Temple of Jerusalem. When they were preparing to rededicate it and light the eternal light in the temple lamp, people found they had only enough oil for one night. Through a miracle, the lamp burned for eight days and nights. The Jews celebrated their religious freedom during this time. Today, families and friends give gifts, tell stories, sing songs, pray, and enjoy special dinners during Hanukkah. The *menorah* is a candleholder for nine candles. The middle candle, the *shammes,* is lit first and used to light the other eight candles—one for each day the holiday is celebrated.

Kwanzaa Kwanzaa in the Swahili language means "first fruit." This seven-day holiday was started in 1966 by Dr. Maulana Ron Karenga to increase the awareness of the African heritage. Although this is a new holiday, the custom of giving thanks for the first fruits and the gifts of nature is an ancient African tradition. Kwanzaa celebrates the black family and is based on seven principles, or themes: unity, self–determination, collective work and responsibility, cooperative economics, creativity, purpose, and faith. Family members wear colorful traditional costumes and cook African foods. They sing and dance to African and African-American music. A woven mat called a *mkeka* is laid on the table and a candle holder, or *kinara,* is placed on it. The kinara has seven candles: three green candles stand for the forests, jungles, and hills of Africa; three red candles symbolize the blood Africans have shed for freedom; and the center black candle symbolizes the dark skin of the people of Africa. Each night a candle is lighted and a theme is discussed. A basket of fruits and vegetables is also placed on the mkeka. The vegetables are a symbol of the harvest, and one ear of corn is laid out for each child in the family. On the last day, small hand-made gifts that reflect affection and time investment, called *zawadi,* are exchanged. Family members then enjoy a special feast called *karamu.* At this time thanks are given for a plentiful harvest, family, friends and community.

©Macmillan/McGraw-Hill

Motion Song

Connection to Language Arts and Music

Songs are a fun part of any celebration. They can also help you remember or summarize important ideas.

> Most any celebration has dance and music. You can write lyrics to go with a favorite tune. The lyrics can be about a person or event that is being celebrated. You can borrow a tune—or compose a tune. You can work in a group to play the tune.

1. Try your hand at composing lyrics and a tune. For starters, celebrate Sir Isaac Newton, his laws of motion and gravitation. Here are some of the words that you want to include in the lyrics:

   Newton

   apple

   gravitation

   acceleration

   motion

   gravity

   law

   action-reaction

   inertia

   force

   velocity

You can add other words that apply. Be sure that your lyrics rhyme. If you start with a tune in mind, you can fit the words into the tune.

2. Once you've given Sir Isaac's song a try, pick a celebration: Tet, Chinese New Year, Diwali, Hanukkah, Kwanzaa, or any other. Decide on key words that you want in your lyrics before you start.

©Macmillan/McGraw-Hill

Mkekas and Measurement

Connection to Math

Measuring skills help prepare the pieces used to weave a ceremonial mat.

A *mkeka* is a colorful ceremonial mat used in Kwanzaa celebrations. In this activity, you will use rulers to measure strips of construction paper. After cutting the strips, you will use them to weave a mkeka.

Procedures

1. Obtain the materials from you teacher.

2. Measure and mark one-inch intervals along the shorter ends of each sheet of paper.

3. Draw lines lengthwise across the papers to connect your marks.

4. Cut along the lines to form long strips. Count the strips.

5. Lay the long green strips in a row across the cardboard. Secure one end of each strip with tape.

6. Weave the short strips over and under the long strips. Use the colors to create a pattern you like. Glue the ends.

7. What is the total area of your mat? _____

   The perimeter? _____

Materials

- 1 sheet of 18 in. x 12 in. green construction paper
- 2 sheets of 9 in. x 12 in. construction paper, one red, one black
- 1 piece of 18 in. x 12 in. thin cardboard
- tape
- ruler
- scissors
- glue

©Macmillan/McGraw - Hill

Cross Curricular
Activity 4

Holiday Writings

Connection to Language Arts

Language arts skills help you communicate your thoughts and ideas.

> The holiday of Kwanzaa takes place over seven days. Each day family members gather to light a candle and discuss a theme. The themes include unity, self-determination, collective work and responsibility, cooperative economics, creativity, purpose, and faith.
>
>
>
> The holiday of Tet, or the Vietnamese New Year, is also a seven-day festival. One of the activities during this time is writing poems. *Cau doi* are poems about the importance of the family. They are written on red strips of paper and hung in the home.

Procedures

1. Choose one of the themes of Kwanzaa that you feel is important to you. Write a letter to a friend or family member. Explain the theme, why it is important to you, and how you would like to address it in your daily life.

2. Trade letters with a classmate that has chosen a different theme. Read each other's letters and discuss the themes you chose. Work out a plan for how you can help each other address your chosen themes in your daily lives.

3. Write a *cau doi* poem about the importance of your family.

4. Once you have completed your poem, copy it onto a strip of red paper.

5. Work as a class to create a bulletin board or other display area to hang everyone's poems.

6. Read the displayed poems. How are they similar? How are they different?

©Macmillan/McGraw-Hill

The Colors of Celebrations

Connection to Art

The colors we see are the result of colors of light being reflected and absorbed by objects.

> Many holidays include the use of color. Kwanzaa includes the colors green, red, and black. Independence Day, or the Fourth of July, use decorations with colors red, white, and blue. Gifts of money wrapped in red paper are given to children by their parents on the Chinese New Year. Poems about the family are written on strips of red paper during the celebration of Tet, the Vietnamese New Year.
>
> All the colors of the spectrum can be created by mixing different amounts of the primary colors of light—red, green, and blue. Some other colors are created when only two of the colors mix. Pigments in objects reflect some colors but absorb others. The absorbed colors are missing in the reflected light. The colors we see are the reflected colors.

Use what you have learned about the colors of light to complete the table.

The Colors of Celebrations			
Color	Celebration	Absorbed Color(s) of Light	Reflected Color(s) of Light
green	Kwanzaa		
red			
blue			
white			
black			

©Macmillan/McGraw-Hill

Design a Holiday

Connection to Language Arts and Music
Language arts and music skills can help you design your own holiday.

> In this activity you will design a new holiday that celebrates a particular event. Your celebration should include things that involve sound, such as music and stories, and things that involve light, such as decorations and costumes.

Procedures

1. Use the table to help you organize your thoughts and plans.

2. Work together to write a song to celebrate your holiday. Be sure to describe the importance of the events, sounds, lights, and colors.

3. Present your holiday to your classmates.

Our Holiday	
Holiday Name	
Who Participates	
Reasons for the Celebration	
Lights and What They Mean	
Sounds and What They Mean	
Colors and What They Mean	
Traditions and What They Mean	
Foods and What They Mean	
Decorations and What They Mean	
Costumes and What They Mean	

©Macmillan/McGraw-Hill

Project Theme

Naturalists, pages 1–10

Concepts
- Read for comprehension.
- Identify and calculate dates of events.
- Analyze and decipher identities of plants.
- Summarize key concepts of animals.
- Collect and organize data to keep a plant journal.

Overview In **Alice Eastwood,** students use a biographical context to learn about plants. Students use critical thinking skills to identify causes and effects in a biographical account; estimation and computation skills to match historical dates and events; and language arts skills to identify plants using a key and to write a summary of a reading selection. The unit culminates as students use language arts and art skills to create and keep a plant journal similar to the one kept by Alice Eastwood.

Getting Started Introduce **Alice Eastwood** to students as a naturalist who grew up in the Rocky Mountains and became famous for her knowledge of plants and their environment. If possible, use *Flower Watching with Alice Eastwood* by Michael Elsohn Ross (Carolrhoda Press, 1997).

Grade 5 Unit A: Structure of Plants and Animals	Activity	Related Subject	Macmillan/McGraw-Hill Programs	Materials
Chapter 1: Plants and Their Parts **Lesson 1:** Classifying Living Things	**Activity 1:** About Alice Eastwood, p. 1	Reading	*McGraw-Hill Reading,* Grade 5, *Lemon Tree,* p.16; *An Island Scrap-book,* science nonfiction,pp. 434–459	
Chapter 1: Plants and Their Parts **Lesson 2:** Roots, Stems, and Leaves	**Activity 2:** Tree Ring Dates, p. 3	Social Studies, Math	*United States: Adventures in Time and Place,* p. 313, 598, 149–150, 178, 619, 106, 259, 230, 635, R50, R46. *McGraw-Hill Mathematics,* Grade 5, elapsed time, pp. 346–349	
Chapter 2: Plant Diversity **Lesson 4:** Plants Without Seeds **Lesson 5:** Plants with Seeds	**Activity 3:** Plant Key, p. 5	Language Arts	*McGraw-Hill Language Arts,* Grade 5, Sentences, pp. 2–7; Descriptions, pp. 372–373	
Chapter 3: Animal Diversity **Lesson 8:** Animal Structure and Function **Lesson 9:** Animal Adaptation	**Activity 4:** Animal Puzzle, p. 7	Language Arts	*McGraw-Hill Reading,* Grade 5, *Tonweya and the Eagles,* pp. 556–557; *McGraw-Hill Language Arts,* Grade 5, Descriptions, pp. 372–373	
Chapter 3: Animal Diversity **Lesson 9:** Animal Adaptation	**Activity 5:** A Butterfly Adaptation, p. 9	Reading, Language Arts	*McGraw-Hill Language Arts,* Grade 5, Summarizing, pp. 36–37, 221, 564, 589	
Chapters 1, 2, and 3: All Lessons	**Culminating Activity:** Plant Journal, p. 10	Language Arts, Art	*McGraw-Hill Language Arts,* Grade 5, Note-Taking, pp. 36–37, 64–65, 146–147, 232–233	sketchbook, magnifying lens, art materials

©Macmillan/McGraw-Hill

Scoring Rubric for Integration Activities	
Score	Criteria
4	Accomplished all of the activity's objectives.
3	Accomplished more than half of the activity's objectives.
2	Accomplished less than half of the activity's objectives.
1	Little or no accomplishment of activity's objectives.

Activity 1

Connection to Reading

About Alice Eastwood, page 1

Objective • Identify causes and effects in a biographical account.

Introduce: Discuss what a *naturalist* is. Point out that naturalists study the natural world and use their knowledge to assess the status of ecosystems.

Teach: Introduce Alice Eastwood as a naturalist, botanist, and scientist. Begin by discussing the times in which Alice lived. In the 19th century, female scientists were uncommon and often had a difficult time gaining acceptance and recognition.

Close: Have volunteers explain how they arrived at their answers.

Assessment: Students should be able to identify both causes and effects.

Modification: For students who have difficulty, phrase relationships as questions. For example, state an effect and then ask, *What caused this to happen?* Similarly, state a cause and ask, *What happened as a result of this?* Encourage students to ask similar questions as they read each paragraph.

Answer: **A.** Cause: Alice's mother died and her father could not take care of his children. **B.** Effect: Alice came to Denver. **C.** Cause: It was considered improper for women to wear pants and boots. **D.** Cause: Wallace wanted to learn about the flowers. **E.** Effect: The academy and Alice's flower collection were destroyed. **F.** Cause: Alice noticed how natural fires could help a plant community by "cleansing" an area. **G.** Cause: Alice had contributed so much to botany.

©Macmillan/McGraw-Hill

Activity 2

Connection to Social Studies and Math

Tree Ring Dates, page 3

Objective • Arrange historical events in chronological order using tree rings as a timeline.

Introduce: Discuss how a tree adds a ring during each growing season, marking its age in years. Ask students if they have seen tree rings. If possible, bring in a tree log or photograph in which tree rings are depicted.

Teach: Review a sample date. For example, ask, *When was the Declaration of Independence signed?* Refer students to references to confirm the date. Instruct students to proceed with the other dates in a similar fashion. Stress use of the correct operations in part B.

Close: Have volunteers share their answers.

Assessment: Students should be able to locate historical dates and arrange them in chronological order, and solve computational problems.

Modification: Take some time to review unfamiliar historical events for ESL students. As a class, discuss the significance of each event.

Answers: **A 1.** 1776 **2.** 1939 **3.** 1519 **4.** 1607 **5.** 1963 **6.** 1570 **7.** 1680 **8.** mid 1700s **9.** 1989 **10.** 1901 **11.** 1801 **B 1.** 1879 **2.** 1823 **3.** 923 years old, in 1077 **4.** 223.8 ft **5.** 1844, 344 years old **6.** 2077, 577 **7.** 347.8 ft

Activity 3

Connection to Language Arts

Plant Key, page 5

Objective • Use a key to identify different plants.

Introduce: If possible, bring a key or field guide into class for students to observe. Review the use of the key with examples. Have students consider a real plant or photograph and use its characteristics to proceed through the key. Point out that not all keys are organized in the same way, but all are similar in that they allow the user to identify a specimen.

Teach: Review the use of the key on the page by going through the process step by step, using one of the flowers. Point out that the key provided is specially constructed for the plants shown on the page. Help students realize that the key will help to evaluate information, and then identify the plant.

©Macmillan/McGraw-Hill

Close: Have volunteers share their answers with the class. Encourage them to discuss and resolve any differences they may have.

Assessment: Students should be able to use the key to identify each plant.

Modification: Advanced students can choose plants and write their own keys.

Answer: **Plant 1:** evening primrose **Plant 2:** horsetail **Plant 3:** larch **Plant 4:** field mustard **Plant 5:** rough-fruited cinquefoil **Plant 6:** fern **Plant 7:** moss **Plant 8:** water lily **Plant 9:** bulbous buttercup **Plant 10:** pine tree **Plant 11:** iris **Plant 12:** liverwort

Activity 4

Connection to Language Arts

Animal Puzzle, pages 7–8

Objective • Summarize vocabulary about animal classification in a puzzle.

Introduce: Explain that many naturalists study animals, attempting to classify them by exploring their similarities and differences.

Teach: Review the concept of animal classification into vertebrates and invertebrates. After students complete the sample puzzle, have student groups make their own puzzles.

Close: Have students explain their answers.

Assessment: Students should be able to identify ways that animals can be classified and place animals in groups.

Modification: If possible, have students use cut-out letters or letters from commercially available word games to assemble their own puzzles.

Answers: **Across: 3.** reptilia, **6.** mammalia, **8.** hair, **9.** invertebrates **Down: 1.** milk, **2.** camouflage, **4.** amphibia, **5.** mimicry, **7.** swim, **8.** hybrid

Activity 5

Connection to Reading and Language Arts

A Butterfly Adaptation, page 9

Objective • Read and write a summary about the concept of mimicry.

Introduce: Explain that Bates' discoveries led him to understand that some butterflies have evolved to mimic other butterflies. Explain mimicry and evolution. Illustrate and explain a summary and how to ascertain the main idea of a story.

© Macmillan/McGraw-Hill

Teach: Explain mimicry and camouflage. Ask volunteers to explain where they think the word *mimicry* came from and why it is used to define the behavior of butterflies.

Close: Have students share their summaries. Have them explain why they chose the details they did.

Assessment: Students should be able to show that they understand the concept of mimicry. They should also be able to demonstrate that they understand the difference between mimicry and camouflage.

Modification: Have students research other scientists who were important in discovering how animals behave.

Culminating Activity

Connection to Language Arts and Art

Plant Journal, page 10

Objective • Create and keep a plant observation journal.

Materials: blank booklet or journal, art materials, magnifying lens

Introduce: Discuss the idea of keeping a plant journal. Point out that in Alice Eastwood's day, there were only two ways to record observations: (1) keep a journal, or (2) keep dried, pressed flowers. Stress the importance of making accurate, detailed drawings or photographs and descriptions of each plant.

Teach: If possible, go on a class walk to give students a start on their journals. Encourage students to find as many varieties as possible. Stress accuracy. Inform students that it is against the law to pick flowers and plants in many localities. Provide field guides, keys, and other resources for identification of each plant. Encourage students to use their journals to express thoughts, observations, opinions, and questions. Encourage them to find answers to their questions using reference books or other sources of information.

Close: Have volunteers present entries from their journals to the class.

Assessment: Students should be able to record their observations accurately.

Modification: Return to the same location more than one time to see how plants change over time.

© Macmillan/McGraw-Hill

Project Theme

The Nature Network, pages 11–16

Concepts
- Describe and build a model of the ecosystem.
- Investigate conflicts among niches.
- Use probability to understand relationships between predator and prey.
- Read maps to locate major biomes.
- Organize ideas to design a new game.

Overview In **The Nature Network**, students use a science television program theme to learn about ecosystems. Students use art and language arts skills to build and label a model of an ecosystem; critical thinking skills to make predictions about ecological competition; math skills to play games that model predator-prey interactions; and map skills to locate biomes around the world. The unit culminates as students use research skills to design a game.

Getting Started Introduce the **Nature Network** to students. Have volunteers describe the kinds of programs that a nature network might include.

Grade 5 Unit B: Interactions of Living Things	Activity	Related Subject	Macmillan/McGraw-Hill Programs	Materials
Chapter 4: Ecosystems **Lesson 1:** Living Things and Their Environment	**Activity 1:** Model Ecosystem, p. 11	Art, Language Arts	*McGraw-Hill Language Arts,* Grade 5, Writing Directions, pp. 214–233	assorted art materials, labels
Chapter 4: Ecosystems **Lesson 2:** Food Chains and Food Webs	**Activity 2:** Niche Battles, p. 12	Language Arts	*McGraw-Hill Language Arts,* Grade 5, Opinions, pp. 130–131	
Chapter 5: Populations and Ecosystems **Lesson 4:** How Populations Survive	**Activity 3:** Predators and Prey, pp. 13–14	Math	*McGraw-Hill Mathematics,* Grade 5, Probability, pp. 602–609	cardboard, scissors, paper clips, markers and construction paper of the same 2 colors
Chapter 5: Populations and Ecosystems **Lesson 5:** Biomes	**Activity 4:** Biome Map, p. 15	Social Studies	*The United States: Adventures in Time and Place,* Grade 5, pp. G4, G9, 65, 121, 602–603	
Chapters 4 and 5: All Lessons	**Culminating Activity:** Design a Game, p. 16	Language Arts	*McGraw-Hill Language Arts,* Grade 5, Writing Directions, pp. 214–233	reference sources, art materials

© Macmillan/McGraw-Hill

Cross Curricular

Scoring Rubric for Integration Activities	
Score	**Criteria**
4	Accomplished all of the activity's objectives.
3	Accomplished more than half of the activity's objectives.
2	Accomplished less than half of the activity's objectives.
1	Little or no accomplishment of activity's objectives.

Activity 1

Connection to Art and Language Arts

A Model Ecosystem, page 11

Objective • Identify the key parts of an ecosystem.

Materials: assorted art materials, labels

Introduce: Ask students to name different ecosystems.

Teach: Review the meanings of the science words in the activity. Remind students that the descriptions of their ecosystems should help the reader imagine the places and the things in them.

Close: Review the factors that students chose to evaluate in the models. Discuss the model ecosystems to be included in the television program. Why was each one chosen?

Assessment: Students should be able to identify an ecosystem, represent it with a model, and accurately label and describe the model.

Modification: Students with physical limitations should take a leadership role within the group, helping to organize everyone's efforts.

Activity 2

Connection to Language Arts

Niche Battles, page 12

Objective • Make predictions about how niches change.

Introduce: Discuss how the competition between the green anole and the Cuban anole affected the population and niche of each organism. Then discuss the following situation: A program called "Animal Stars" moves to the same TV time slot as that of "Niche Battles." Both programs feature stories about animals with great photography. How might their TV niche and number of viewers change?

©Macmillan/McGraw - Hill

Teach: Break down each problem into a table. Have students give reasons for each change, then make predictions based on their tables.

Close: Have volunteers present their conclusions.

Assessment: Students should be able to reasonably predict how competition will affect a niche.

Modification: Gifted students may create and solve "niche battle" situations.

Answers: **1.** The Green anole's population and niche should remain unchanged; the Cuban anole's population and niche size will decrease, perhaps moving to middle branches. **2.** Crabgrass will take over the niche of the rye grass because it is faster-growing and heartier. **3.** The hawk population and niche may shrink slightly as owls consume some of their prey. **4.** Trees will take over the niche of shrubs and grasses, blocking sunlight and eventually turning the field into a forest.

Activity 3

Connection to Math

Predators and Prey, pages 13–14

Objective • Use probability to analyze a game.

Materials: cardboard, scissors, paper clips, 2 colors of markers, 2 colors of construction paper to match colors of markers

Introduce: Review the terms *predator* and *prey*. List common predators and prey and discuss their interactions. Point out that a successful predator-prey relationship is one in which both predator and prey can survive in large numbers. Ask, *What will happen if predators are so strong and fast that they eat all the prey in an area?*

Teach: Review the rules of the game and play a sample round. Guide students in their mathematical analysis.

Close: Have students draw conclusions about predator-prey interactions based on the outcomes of the games.

Assessment: Students should see successful predator-prey relationships.

Modification: Students can calculate the probabilities of different outcomes using spinners with fewer or more sections.

Answers: **1.** 1/2; 1/2. **2.** equal; both predators and prey have an equal chance for survival **3.** It is advantageous for both predators and prey to have an equal chance for survival because their relationship can then go on indefinitely. **4.** Eliminating most of the prey is bad for the survival of a predator because it takes away its food source.

©Macmillan/McGraw-Hill

Activity 4

Connection to Social Studies

Biome Map, page 47

Objective	• Interpret a map and map key to answer questions.
Introduce:	Ask student to locate the continent and area on which they live.
Teach:	Review the names and locations of all six populated continents. Review the biomes and discuss the biome in which they live.
Close:	Have volunteers explain their answers.
Assessment:	Students use a map key to identify biomes on a world map.
Modification:	Have students search magazines for pictures of each biome.
Answers:	**1.** North America, Asia, Europe, South America, Africa **2.** Asia, Australia **3.** Australia **4.** Africa, savanna **5.** Asia, North America **6.** Africa

Culminating Activity

Connection to Language Arts

Design a Game, page 48

Objectives	• Design a game based on key ecological principles.
Materials:	reference sources, assorted art materials
Introduce:	Ask students to discuss their favorite games. Make a list. Classify the games into groups such as board games, games of chance, and so on.
Teach:	Form groups of four. The moderators will read the questions and determine the correct answers. Remind students that their instructions should present information in a logical time order and explain how something is made or done.
Close:	Encourage all students to play the new games. Ask them to vote on the best games in different categories and explain their choices.
Assessment:	Students should be able to design games that cover unit topics.
Modification:	Allow ESL students to give answers in any form.
Answers:	**Down–Blackland:** digging, from the soil, buffalo, grass; **Producers:** oxygen, carbon dioxide, break down dead material, make food; **Parts:** abiotic factors, biotic factors, population, habitat; **You Are:** omnivore, herbivore, carnivore, prey

©Macmillan/McGraw-Hill

Cross Curricular

Project Theme

Geo-Explorers, pages 7–24

Concepts
- Calculate the distance planets travel around the Sun.
- Study a map to locate earthquake zones.
- Read and pay close attention to details.
- Make calculations to explore water waste over periods of time.
- Read and interpret graphs.
- Write a letter to persuade others.

Overview In **Geo-Explorers**, students use an exploration club theme to learn about Earth and its resources. Students use math skills to calculate and compare orbit sizes of planets, to determine how much water is wasted by a leaky faucet, and to interpret circle graphs of energy use; social studies skills to locate earthquake zones; reading skills to solve science mysteries; and language arts skills to keep an environmental diary. The unit culminates with students writing persuasive letters responding to a contest searching for new Geo-Explorers.

Getting Started Introduce students to Hank Hudson and his **Geo-Explorers**. Ask students to think of activities that the Geo-Explorers might undertake and what kinds of adventures they would have.

Grade 5 Unit C: Earth and Its Resources	Activity	Related Subject	Macmillan/McGraw-Hill Programs	Materials
Chapter 6: Rocks and Minerals **Lesson 1:** Earth and Its Neighbors	**Activity 1:** Hank Hudson, Geo-Explorer, p. 17	Math	*McGraw-Hill Mathematics,,* Grade 5, Multiple Whole Numbers by Decimals, pp. 70–73	calculator (optional)
Chapter 6: Rocks and Minerals **Lesson 2:** Earth's Changing Crust	**Activity 2:** Earthquake Map, p. 19	Social Studies	*The United States: Adventures in Time and Place,* Grade 5, pp. G6, G9, R14–15	world map
Chapter 6: Rocks and Minerals **Lesson 3:** Minerals of Earth's Crust **Lesson 4:** Earth's Rocks and Soil	**Activity 3:** Hank's Tricky Mysteries, p. 21	Reading	*McGraw-Hill Reading,* Grade 5 *Digging Up the Past,* pp. 244–248 *McGraw-Hill Reading,* Grade 5 *A Mountain of a Monument,* pp. 374–378	
Chapter 7: Air, Water, and Energy **Lesson 6:** Earth's Fresh Water **Lesson 7:** Earth's Oceans	**Activity 4:** Water Waste, p. 22	Math	*McGraw-Hill Mathematics,* Grade 5, Time, pp. 346–349; Rates, pp. 592–595	calibrated containers, clock or timer, opt calculator
Chapter 7: Air, Water, and Energy **Lessons 8:** Energy Resources	**Activity 5:** Energy Graphs, p. 23	Math, Social Studies	*McGraw-Hill Mathematics,* Grade 5, Circle Graphs; pp. 652–655; *The United States: Adventures in Time and Place,* Gr. 5, pp. 42–48	
Chapters 6 and 7: All Lessons	**Culminating Activity:** Be a Geo-Explorer Contest, p. 24	Language Arts	*McGraw-Hill Language Arts,* Grade 5, Persuasive Writing, pp. 126–145; Letters; pp. 129, 137, 140–147	

©Macmillan/McGraw-Hill

Cross Curricular

Scoring Rubric for Integration Activities	
Score	**Criteria**
4	Accomplished all of the activity's objectives.
3	Accomplished more than half of the activity's objectives.
2	Accomplished less than half of the activity's objectives.
1	Little or no accomplishment of activity's objectives.

Activity 1

Connection to Math

Hank Hudson, Geo-Explorer, pages 17–18

Objective • Use estimation and computation skills to calculate and compare orbit sizes of planets.

Materials: calculator (optional)

Introduce: Refer students to the chart on page C7 of their science text showing the length of years on different planets. Point out that planets farther from the Sun have larger orbits than closer planets.

Teach: Review multiplying 2-digit, 3-digit, and greater numbers. Explain that the distance of each planet's orbit can be calculated by multiplying its distance from the Sun by 6.3. (This is a simplified version of the formula Circumference = π x diameter.) Have students express all answers in millions and round to the nearest whole. Ask a volunteer to demonstrate how to solve the first problem. Encourage students to estimate the answers first.

Close: Have volunteers present their answers to the class.

Assessment: Students should be able to find approximate orbit distances using the given formula.

Modification: Students may wish to check their answers with a calculator.

Answers: **1.** 36 million miles, 227 million miles **2.** Mercury: 227; Venus: 422; Earth: 586; Mars: 895; Jupiter: 3,043; Saturn: 5,582; Uranus: 11,233; Neptune: 17,596; Pluto: 23,096 **3.** Mercury; Pluto **4.** 309 million miles **5.** Earth by 359 million miles **6.** Saturn by 5,160 million miles **7.** 1,172 million miles **8.** Two orbits of Earth, by 277 million miles **9.** Jupiter, by 113 million miles **10.** Pluto, by 768 million miles

©Macmillan/McGraw-Hill

Cross Curricular

Activity 2

Connection to Social Studies

Earthquake Map, pages 19–20

Objectives • Identify earthquake zones on the globe.
• Use directions to find locations on a map.

Introduce: Discuss how faults in Earth's moving plates create places where earthquakes occur.

Teach: Review cardinal and intermediate directions and how to read a political map. Tell students to draw a thick band on the map to identify each earthquake zone.

Close: Have volunteers identify earthquake zones.

Assessment: Students should be able to use a description to find a map location.

Modification: Use a relief map to allow sight-impaired students to participate in the activity.

Answers: Maps should depict the earthquake bands described on the page.

Activity 3

Connection to Reading

Hank's Tricky Mysteries, page 21

Objectives • Identify properties of rocks and minerals.
• Read critically to find information to solve problems.

Introduce: Review Moh's scale, formation of coal, the streak test, crystal formation, and contour plowing.

Teach: Go over a sample mystery from the page. For example, in the first mystery, only the bituminous coal location was likely a swamp in the past. It would be the logical choice for finding crocodile fossils.

Close: Have volunteers explain their solutions.

Assessment Students should be able to draw conclusions from the evidence given.

Modification: Make a list of clues and their implications for students who are having trouble. Give additional clues, if necessary.

Answers: **1.** bituminous coal location **2.** D, C, B, A **3.** Iron pyrite is yellow but leaves a greenish black streak, so it may have scratched the fender. **4.** Lainee is right because larger crystals are more likely to have formed underground. **5.** The east side farmer probably prevented erosion by contour plowing.

©Macmillan/McGraw-Hill

Activity 4

Connection to Math

Water Waste, page 22

Objectives • Measure the amount of water wasted by a leaky faucet.
• Make multi-step calculations.

Materials: quart, gallon, or other calibrated containers, a clock, watch or timer, calculator (optional)

Introduce: Ask students, *How much water do you think a dripping faucet wastes in one year?* Write the students' estimates on the board. Then tell them that they will calculate how much water a dripping faucet actually wastes.

Teach: Review multiplying 2-digit, 3-digit, and greater numbers. Review capacity in customary and metric units. Distribute gallon containers (or other calibrated container sizes). Tell students to collect water for the period of time that you designate (15 minutes, etc.). Go through a sample calculation: 2 gallons per 1 hour → 48 gallons per day → 336 gallons per week → 1,344 gallons per month → 16,128 gallons per year.

Close: Compare the students' predictions to actual data collected.

Assessment: Students should be able to make accurate measurements and calculations, and analyze their data.

Modification: Disabled students may need assistance in manipulating materials.

Answers: Answers will vary. Typical response: about 2 gallons per hour or 16,000 gallons per year.

©Macmillan/McGraw-Hill

Cross Curricular

Activity 5

Connection to Math and Social Studies

Energy Graphs, pages 23–24

Objective • Interpret energy use data from circle graphs.

Introduce: Discuss energy use in the United States. Ask students to predict which country or region uses the most energy.

Teach: Review how to compare fractions and to interpret a circle graph. Then review both graphs with students. Ask questions such as, *The United States uses about how many times as much energy as Asia?* Students should be able to estimate that the United States uses more than twice as much energy as Asia.

Close: Discuss students' answers.

Culminating Activity

Connection to Language Arts

Be a Geo-Explorer Contest, page 24

Objective • Write a persuasive letter to enter a contest.

Introduce: Ask students to think about and discuss the types of things they would like to explore as Geo-Explorers.

Teach: Remind students that a persuasive letter is composed to convince the reader to share the writer's opinion, facts, and practical ideas to argue a point. Review the steps of the writing process: prewriting, drafting, revising, proofreading, and publishing. Provide paper for students to write their letters.

Close: Have students read their letters in class and follow steps 4–5 on the activity sheet.

Assessment: Students should be able to write clear and convincing letters that are scientifically accurate.

Modification: ESL students can make posters depicting the types of adventures they would like to have as a Geo-Explorer and what personal characteristics would contribute to making them good Geo-Explorers.

Project Theme

The Galveston Hurricane of 1900, pages 25–32

Concepts
- Summarize to understand a historical event.
- Map locations using data.
- Analyze tables and charts to compare hurricanes.
- Read for comprehension.
- Collect and organize data to create a hurricane report.

Overview In The **Galveston Hurricane of 1900**, students use a hurricane theme to learn about weather and climate. Students use critical-reading skills to analyze the history of the storm; map-reading skills to follow the path of the storm; graph-reading skills to compare different hurricanes; and critical-reading skills to use context clues to determine the meanings of new words and make inferences from Galveston survivor stories. The unit culminates as students use art, writing, and data-collection skills to make a report on a hurricane.

Getting Started Introduce **The Galveston Hurricane of 1900** to students as one of the worst disasters of the 20th century. Ask students to talk about recent hurricanes with which they are familiar. Where do hurricanes strike? (Over warm tropical oceans near the equator) During what time of the year do hurricanes strike? (Late summer through mid-fall)

Grade 5 Unit D: Weather and Climate	Activity	Related Subject	Macmillan/McGraw-Hill Programs	Materials
Chapter 9: Weather Patterns and Climate **Lesson 5:** Air Masses and Fronts **Lesson 6:** Severe Storms	**Activity 1:** Storm of the Century, p. 25	Reading, Language Arts	*McGraw-Hill Reading,* Grade 5, *The Big Storm,* pp. 466–487, *McGraw-Hill Language Arts,* Grade 5, Summarizing, pp. 36–37, 221, 564, 589	wall map, labels
Chapter 9: Weather Patterns and Climate **Lesson 5:** Air Masses and Fronts **Lesson 6:** Severe Storms	**Activity 2:** Tracking the Storm, p. 27	Social Studies	*United States: Adventures in Time and Place,* Grade 5, pp. G4–G7, 40–41, 336–337	
Chapter 9: Weather Patterns and Climate **Lesson 6:** Severe Storms	**Activity 3:** Comparing Hurricanes, p. 29	Math	*McGraw-Hill Mathematics,* Grade 5, Bar Graphs, pp. 160–163	
Chapter 9: Weather Patterns and Climate **Lesson 6:** Severe Storms	**Activity 4:** Survivor Stories, p. 30	Reading	*McGraw-Hill Reading,* Grade 5, *The Big Storm,* pp. 466–488 *Read a Weather Map,* p. 490	
Chapters 8 and 9: All Lessons	**Culminating Activity:** Hurricane Report, p. 32	Language Arts, Social Studies, Art	*McGraw-Hill Reading,* Grade 5, *Tornadoes!,* pp. 126–130; *United States: Adventures in Time and Place,* Grade 5, pp. G4–G7, 40–41, 336–337	

©Macmillan/McGraw-Hill

Cross Curricular

Scoring Rubric for Integration Activities	
Score	**Criteria**
4	Accomplished all of the activity's objectives.
3	Accomplished more than half of the activity's objectives.
2	Accomplished less than half of the activity's objectives.
1	Little or no accomplishment of activity's objectives.

Activity 1

Connection to Reading

Storm of the Century, pages 25–26

Objective • Summarize key ideas.

Introduce: Show a map of the Gulf of Mexico and Caribbean. Then ask, *Which areas on the map might need to worry about hurricanes?* Students should infer that coastal areas are most likely to be hit by hurricanes. Locate Galveston. Point out that the Galveston hurricane is considered to be one of the century's worst disasters not because of its size, but because its deadly toll—damaging nearly every building on the island and killing some 8,000 people out of a population of close to 38,000. The extent of destruction had two primary causes: (1) Galveston's location made it a prime target for gulf storms, and (2) Galveston's infrastructure offered little protection from the storm. Houses on the island were generally flimsy. Escape routes to the mainland were precarious, and without a sea wall, Galveston's elevation of 8.7 feet above sea level made it possible for a large hurricane to completely inundate the island.

Teach: Have one volunteer read the first paragraph aloud, and ask another to summarize the paragraph. Stress that each summary should get to the main idea of the paragraph, as well as any other important information that the paragraph contains.

Close: Have volunteers read their summary sentences to the class and discuss and resolve any differences.

Assessment: For each summary, ask, *Does the summary give a good idea of the information in the paragraph?* If not, students should reevaluate the paragraph and write a new summary.

Modification: Have students use their summary sentences to create a summary of the entire passage. Students should add transitional sentences if necessary.

Answers: 1. The city of Galveston was destroyed by a hurricane and thousands of people were killed in September of 1900. **2.** Galveston was an

©Macmillan/McGraw-Hill

island that was only a few feet above sea level and some people were concerned about what might happen if a big storm hit. **3.** Dr. Cline warned people of the storm, but few left the island. **4.** Two weather systems created huge waves before the storm, which would soon trap Galveston's residents. **5.** The island plunged into darkness and destruction. **6.** People did what they could to survive the storm, which lasted about eight hours. **7.** While destruction on the island was almost total, people worked hard to rebuild Galveston.

Activity 2

Connection to Social Studies

Tracking the Storm, pages 27–28

Objective • Track the path of a storm on a map and solve problems using a map scale.

Materials: wall map, labels

Introduce: Review map concepts, including compass points, longitude, and latitude. Show that longitudes are designated in degrees East and West, such as 20° E or 90° W. Have students locate sample longitudes on a map. Repeat the process for latitude (e.g. 30° N). Then have students use their estimation skills to find longitudes and latitudes that are "between the lines" such as 17° N or 62° W. Review how to use a scale to estimate distances.

Teach: Refer students to the map on the activity sheet. Call attention to the longitude and latitude lines shown. Then locate the first storm position—15° N and 63° W. Have a volunteer show how to locate this point on the wall map. Confirm that 15° N and 63° W is located in the Windward Islands. Then, point out the map's scale. Show that each unit length can be translated into miles. (Bring to attention that the scale provided on the activity sheet may differ from that on the wall map.) Give several examples. Have students estimate mileage on the map using a scale. Then have students complete the activity.

Close: Have groups compare their answers to step 3 and work together to resolve any differences they may have.

Assessment: Students should be able to find locations on a map using longitude, latitude, and map scale.

Modification: Use a strip of paper to make a scale for students who have trouble using scales. Mark off end points of the scale on the strip. Then show how to use the strip to mark off mileage on the map.

Answers: These are estimates. **3a.** 1,100 miles **3b.** 875 miles **3c.** 2,000 miles

©Macmillan/McGraw-Hill

Cross Curricular

Activity 3

Connection to Math

Comparing Hurricanes, page 29

Objective • Use a table and a bar graph to solve problems.

Introduce: Introduce the hurricane scale, known as the Saffir-Simpson scale, which rates hurricanes on the basis of wind speed, storm wave (officially known as a *storm surge*, the size of the wave produced by the hurricane), and damage. Point out that values in the scale are not absolute, as unusual conditions may cause a parameter to fall outside the normal range. This occurred with the Galveston hurricane, as its winds of 120+ mph rated it a Category 3 hurricane, while its storm wave fell in line with a Category 4 storm.

Teach: Review the hurricane scale. Emphasize that students need to use the table and graph together to find information needed to solve the problems.

Close: Have volunteers present their solutions to the class.

Assessment: Students should solve problems using a table and graph.

Modification: Have students invent data for fictional hurricanes and create problems to solve using their data.

Answers: **1.** Georges, 13-18 ft **2.** Mitch; its winds were about 60 mph faster than the Galveston hurricane **3.** 3.7 ft **4.** Earl; Category 1 **5.** 165 mph

Activity 4

Connection to Reading

Survivor Stories, pages 30–31

Objective • Use context clues to infer the meanings of words and situations.

Introduce: Set the scene for students on the evening of September 8th. The island was without lights and completely covered with water. Winds whipped at a speed of over 120 mph. All escape routes to the mainland were washed out. Ask, *What would you have done?* Record students' responses.

Teach: Work with the class to answer the first survivor account. Show how to infer information from the context. For vocabulary based questions, remind students that one way to figure out the meaning of a word's usage is to look for clues or its definition in nearby words and sentences.

Close: Have volunteers share their inferences with the class.

© Macmillan/McGraw-Hill

Cross Curricular

Assessment: Students should be able to use context clues to infer definitions and answer questions.

Modification: Have advanced students categorize unfamiliar words by type. Ask, *Is the word a noun? Verb? Adjective? Adverb?* Encourage students to use these clues to infer the meaning of other unfamiliar words.

Answers: **The Boss Family's Story:** *hurtled*–moved with great speed; *cistern*–A structure that collects and holds water. **Mr. Fewell's Story:** *unscathed*–unhurt or unharmed; He was fearful for his life. **The Irwin Family's Story:** *refuge*–shelter or protection; floating on the roof. **Mr. Frost's Story:** *dislocated*–A joint that has come apart; He was stranded on a beach when the storm hit, but he survived and no one knew where he finally landed. **Mr. Lundwall's Story:** *moorings*–things that hold a harbored boat in place; The ship is touching or resting on the ground.

Culminating Activity

Connection to Language Arts, Social Studies, and Art

Hurricane Report, page 31

Objective • Collect and analyze data for a report.

Introduce: Tell students that every hurricane has its own unique story, similar to that of the Galveston hurricane. Assemble resources for students to use for research—books, magazines, and other print materials. The Internet is especially useful for hurricane research. Provide paper for students to write their reports.

Teach: Help groups organize their information. Stress that reports tell a story in words, pictures, and by using charts, graphs, and maps. Explain that a report should include an introduction, a body, and a conclusion. Remind students that the facts and figures they use should be accurate. Review the steps of the writing process: prewriting, drafting, revising, proofreading, and publishing.

Close: Have volunteers display their reports in class and compare them.

Assessment: Reports should be organized, accurate, and clearly presented.

Modification: Allow students to present their reports orally to the class.

©Macmillan/McGraw-Hill

Project Theme

Matter Magazine, pages 33–40

Concepts
- Understand the relationship between mass and weight.
- Explore the importance of Dmitry Mendeleyev's contribution to chemistry.
- Read, interpret, and compare graphs.
- Identify foods as compounds or specific types of mixtures.
- Use characteristics of matter to solve a practical problem by planning, designing, and drawing an invention.

Overview In *Matter Magazine*, students use a magazine format to explore relationships between matter and energy. Students use: computational skills to compute and compare weights of objects on the Moon and planets; reading skills to understand an article about a scientist; spatial skills to interpret graphs; and classification skills to identify different forms of matter. The unit culminates as students use their language arts and art skills to design a new invention.

Getting Started Introduce students to *Matter Magazine*, the magazine that is all about matter. Encourage students to suggest the kinds of articles this magazine might publish. Make a list of the topics on the board.

Grade 5 Unit E: Properties of Matter and Energy	Activity	Related Subject	Macmillan/McGraw-Hill Programs
Chapter 10: Properties and Structure of Matter **Lesson 1:** Physical Properties	**Activity 1:** Bowling in Space, p. 33	Math	*McGraw-Hill Mathematics*, Grade 5, Multiple Whole Numbers by Decimals, pp. 70–73
Chapter 10: Properties and Structure of Matter **Lesson 2:** What Matter Is Made Of	**Activity 2:** Dmitry Mendeleyev, p. 35	Reading	*Spotlight on Literacy*, Grade 5, <u>Scenes of Wonder</u>, pp. 25, 81, 85, 105, 109; *McGraw-Hill Reading*, Grade 5, *The Gold Coin*, pp. 140–162
Chapter 10: Properties and Structure of Matter Lesson 3: Solids, Liquids, and Gases	**Activity 3:** Water Graphs, p. 36	Math	*McGraw-Hill Mathematics*, Grade 5 Line Graphs, pp. 166–169 Temperature, pp. 374–375
Chapter 11: Forms of Matter and Energy **Lesson 4:** Mixtures and Solutions	**Activity 4:** What's the Ingredient?, p. 38	Health	*McGraw-Hill Health*, Grade 5, Chapter 5, pp. 111–139
Chapters 10 and 11: All Lessons	**Culminating Activity:** Invention Contest, p. 39	Language Arts, Art	*McGraw-Hill Language Arts*, Grade 5, Brainstorming, pp. 132–133, Expository Writing, pp. 300–319

© Macmillan/McGraw-Hill

Scoring Rubric for Integration Activities	
Score	Criteria
4	Accomplished all of the activity's objectives.
3	Accomplished more than half of the activity's objectives.
2	Accomplished less than half of the activity's objectives.
1	Little or no accomplishment of activity's objectives.

Activity 1

Connection to Math

Bowling in Space, pages 33–34

Objectives • Understand the relationship between mass and weight.
• Multiply using decimal numbers.

Introduce: Discuss the difference between mass and weight. Explain that the Moon has less mass than Earth. Therefore, the pull of gravity on the Moon is less than on Earth. This causes an object to weigh one-sixth (0.167) as much on the Moon as it does on Earth. Point out that while an object weighs different amounts on different celestial bodies, its mass remains unchanged.

Teach: Have a volunteer find the weight of an object on the Moon by multiplying the object's weight in newtons by 0.167 ($\frac{1}{6}$). Thus, a 120-newton bowling ball on the Moon weighs: 120 x 0.167 = 20 newtons. Remind students to insert the decimal point. Review the use of a number line to compare and order numbers. Students can round to the nearest newton.

Close: Make a chart on the chalkboard. Have volunteers fill in the chart.

Assessment: Students should recognize the difference between mass and weight and understand how to multiply with decimals.

Modification: Advanced students can check other students' calculations without using calculators.

Answers: **1.** Weight Chart (rounded to nearest newton) Earth (answers given as sample); Moon: 20 N; 3 N; 78 N; Mars: 46 N; 8 N; 179 N; Jupiter: 317 N; 53 N; 1,241 N, Saturn: 139 N; 23 N; 545 N **2.** From least to greatest: pin on the Moon (3 N); pin on Mars (8 N); pin on Earth (20 N); ball on the Moon (20 N); pin on Saturn (23 N); ball on Mars (46 N); pin on Jupiter (53 N); person on the Moon (78 N); ball on Earth (120 N); ball on Saturn (139 N); person on Mars (179 N); ball on Jupiter (317 N); person on Earth (470 N); person on Saturn (545 N); person on Jupiter (1,241 N). Any given object weighs most on Jupiter and least on the Moon.

©Macmillan/McGraw-Hill

Activity 2

Connection to Reading

Dmitry Mendeleyev, page 35

Objectives • Explore the importance of Dmitry Mendeleyev's contribution to chemistry.
• Read to find the main idea, use context clues, make inferences, draw conclusions, and summarize information.

Introduce: Assess prior knowledge by asking students to discuss what they know about Dmitry Mendeleyev and the periodic table of the elements.

Teach: Review with students how to identify the main idea of a passage, use context clues to find the meanings of new words, make inferences, draw conclusions, and to summarize information they have read. Provide paper for students to write their responses.

Close: Have volunteers explain their answers to the questions.

Assessment: Students should be able to answer the questions correctly and provide an accurate summary of the passage.

Modification: Have students make an outline of the passage to help them organize the information.

Answers: **1.** The main idea is that Dmitry Mendeleyev developed the basis for the modern periodic table of the elements. **2.** Periodic: repeating in a certain pattern; atomic number: the number of protons in an atom of a specific element **3.** The elements can be arranged based on their atomic number in a periodic, or repeating, pattern. **4.** Accept all reasonable and accurate summaries.

Activity 3

Connection to Math

Water Graphs, pages 36–37

Objective • Read, interpret, and compare temperature data on graphs.

Introduce: Tell students that as altitude increases, the air becomes thinner and air pressure decreases. This thin air presses down with less force on the liquid water surface. This allows water particles to escape from the surface more easily, and thus boil at a lower temperature. Ask, *Can this lower temperature be measured?* Have students look at the graphs to find out.

© Macmillan/McGraw-Hill

Cross Curricular

Teach: Review the sea level graph. At 0°C the container is filled with ice. The temperature remains at 0°C until all the ice is melted. The temperature starts to rise after the ice changes completely to liquid. The temperature stops rising at 100°C, as now all energy is given to changing the state from liquid to gas.

Close: Have volunteers present their answers to the class.

Assessment: Students should be able to identify the state of water at each point on the graph and find the corresponding temperature.

Modification: Visual learners should be helped by drawing diagrams next to each stage on the graph. For example, as the water nears its melting point, you can draw a container that is filled with both liquid water and ice.

Answers: **1.** About 18 minutes **2.** 0–18 minutes **3.** 18–40 minutes **4.** After 40 minutes **5.** Sea level: 100°C; high altitude: 96°C **6.** Sea level: 100°C; high altitude: 96°C **7.** 4°C lower at high altitude **8.** The heavier sea level air places more pressure on the water's surface. This makes it harder for water particles to escape as gas. **9.** Below 96°C **10.** Air pressure differences

Activity 4

Connection to Health

What's the Ingredient?, page 38

Objective • Identify foods as compounds or specific types of mixtures.

Introduce: Have volunteers define the terms compound, solution, suspension, and colloid. Point out that all mixtures can be separated by physical means—filters, settling, evaporation, distillation, and dissolving. Compounds can only be separated by chemical change.

Teach: Review the first item. Cool River is not a compound because it can be separated by physical means (evaporation). The drink is not a colloid since it does not scatter light. The drink is not a suspension because it does not settle out. The drink is a solution because it is clear and can only be separated by evaporation.

Close: Have volunteers explain their answers.

Assessment: Students should be able to distinguish compounds from mixtures and identify different kinds of mixtures.

Modification: Have students make a checklist or flowchart that they can refer to that asks questions to help them identify each substance. For example, it can ask: *Can the substance be separated by a filter? Evaporation? Settling?* The answer to each question would then refer

©Macmillan/McGraw-Hill

students to another question, finally arriving at an identification.

Answers: **A.** Cool River: solution. **B.** Super Sauce: suspension.
C. Sweet Crystals: compound. **D.** Swell Gel: colloid.

Culminating Activity

Connection to Language Arts and Art

Invention Contest, page 39

Objectives: • Use characteristics of matter to solve a practical problem.
• Plan, design, and draw an invention.

Materials: drawing materials

Introduce: Use the table provided to discuss various inventions with the class. Focus on the need that each invention filled. For example, ask: *What need does the safety pin fill?* Students should be able to recognize a variety of uses for a safety pin and the fact that once it is closed it cannot easily spring open and that the sharp point is covered once the pin is closed.

Teach: Help groups think of ideas for their inventions. Focus on the properties of matter that make each invention work. For example, light, flexible metal makes safety pins successful.

Close: Hold an "Invention Fair" where students can display their creations.

Assessment: Inventions should be creative and attempt to solve a real-world problem.

Modification: Encourage students to choose an invention from the table and to research the process of its invention and the inventor.

©Macmillan/McGraw-Hill

Cross Curricular

Project Theme

Celebrate with Movement, Sound, and Light, pages 41–47

Concepts
- Read for comprehension.
- Summarize concepts of motion.
- Measure and use patterns to create a ceremonial mat.
- Communicate and organize ideas into a poem.
- Analyze information to complete a table.
- Organize data to design a holiday for an event.

Overview In **Celebrate with Movement, Sound, and Light**, students follow the importance of movement, sound, and light in celebrations in different cultures around the world. Students use reading skills to learn about different holidays; language arts skills to summarize ideas; math skills to create a ceremonial mat; language art skills to write poems; and art skills to analyze the colors used in many celebrations. The unit culminates as students create their own holidays.

Getting Started Introduce **Celebrate with Movement, Sound, and Light** by asking students what holidays they celebrate. Discuss the traditions associated with each holiday. Ask about the sounds and light in each holiday.

Grade 5 Unit F: Motion and Energy	Activity	Related Subject	Macmillan/McGraw-Hill Programs	Materials
Chapter 13: Sound Energy **Lesson 5:** Pitch and Loudness	**Activity 1:** Celebrations Around the World, p. 41	Reading	*McGraw-Hill Language Arts,* Grade 5, *Writing That Compares,* pp. 380–396	
Chapter 13: Sound Energy **Lesson 5:** Pitch and Loudness	**Activity 2:** Motion Song, p. 43	Language Arts, Music	*McGraw-Hill Language Arts,* Grade 5, *Writing Poems,* pp. 154–155, 589; *McGraw-Hill Reading,* Grade 5, *The Sidewalk Racer,* p. 254; *How to Think Like a Scientist,* pp. 410-428; Use an Outline, p. 430	Classroom instruments, recording equipment
Chapter 14: Light Energy **Lesson 9:** Light and Color	**Activity 3:** Mkekas and Measurement, p. 44	Math	*McGraw-Hill Mathematics,* Grade 5, Length, pp. 350–353; Perimeter, pp. 540–541; Area, pp. 542–545	sheet of 18-in. x 12 in. green construction paper, red and black sheets of 9-in. x 12 in. construction, paper, piece of 18-in. x 12 in. thin cardboard, ruler, scissors, glue, tape
Chapter 14: Light Energy **Lesson 9:** Light and Color	**Activity 4:** Holiday Writings, p. 45	Language Arts	*McGraw-Hill Language Arts,* Grade 5, Expository Writing, pp. 302–318	red strips of paper paper 6-in. x 12-in.
Chapter 14: Light Energy **Lesson 9:** Light and Color	**Activity 5:** The Colors of Celebrations, p. 46	Art		
Chapters 12, 13, and 14: All Lessons	**Culminating Activity:** Design a Holiday, p. 47	Language Arts, Music	*Share the Music,* Grade 5, Celebrations, pp. 316–371	

©Macmillan/McGraw-Hill

Cross Curricular

Scoring Rubric for Integration Activities	
Score	Criteria
4	Accomplished all of the activity's objectives.
3	Accomplished more than half of the activity's objectives.
2	Accomplished less than half of the activity's objectives.
1	Little or no accomplishment of activity's objectives.

Activity 1

Connection to Reading

Celebrations Around the World, pages 41–42

Objective • Recognize use of color, light, and sound in cultural celebrations.

Introduce: Have students brainstorm celebrations. Ask, *What types of color, lights, and sounds are associated with each celebration?* Tell students that they will learn about other celebrations around the world, and their colors, lights, and sounds.

Teach: Review how to identify the main idea and its supporting details. Help students create a table to compare and contrast two holidays. Possible headers: *Holiday; What does it celebrate?; Who celebrates it?; What colors are important?; How is light used?; How is sound used?*

Close: Have students present their comparisons to the class.

Assessment: Students should recognize that sound and light in the form of music, fireworks, and colors are often important in celebrating holidays.

Modification: Invite students to share information about other celebrations.

Activity 2

Connection to Language Arts and Music

Motion Song

Objective • Summarize main ideas about motion in a song.
• Use concepts of pitch in composing the tune.

Introduce: Have students recite lyrics of familiar tunes to review rhyming.

Teach: Have students define the list of words to use in the Sir Isaac Newton song. Then assemble groups of students and suggest roles within each group—lyricist, composer, player, recorder.

©Macmillan/McGraw-Hill

Close: Have students share and record their tunes on tape recorders.

Assessment: Students should be able to explain the lyrics of their tunes.

Modification: Students might write poems without any particular tune in mind.

Answers: Answers will vary depending on students' cooperative efforts as well as an accurate use of terms considering definitions and applications.

Activity 3

Connection to Math

Mkekas and Measurement, page 44

Objective • Use linear measure to weave a ceremonial mat.

Materials: green sheet of 18-in. x 12-in. construction paper, red and black sheets of 9-in. x 12-in. construction paper, 18-in. x 12-in. thin cardboard, ruler, scissors, glue, tape

Introduce: Discuss the Kwanzaa. Invite students who celebrate the holiday to describe it. If anyone owns a mkeka, ask them to bring it to class.

Teach: Review how to make linear measurements. Then explain warp and weft in weaving. The warp equals the long strips which form the base. These will be one color. The weft equals the short strips which are woven. These will be two different colors. Demonstrate making a mkeka and the different patterns that result if you vary the placement of the colored strips.

Close: Students can hold a Kwanzaa celebration. Have them make kinaras from construction paper and set the mat with paper fruit and vegetables. Students can talk about the themes of the Kwanzaa.

Assessment: Students should be able to follow instructions to weave the mat.

Modification: For students with physical disabilities, have the strips already cut and taped to the poster board so he/she can concentrate on weaving the mat.

Answers: 7. Area = 216 square inches, perimeter = 60 inches

©Macmillan/McGraw-Hill

Cross Curricular

Activity 4

Connection to Language Arts

Holiday Writings, page 45

Objective • Express your thoughts and feelings about a theme of Kwanzaa.

Materials: red strips of paper 6-in. x 12-in.

Introduce: Discuss holidays students celebrate with their families. What meaningful traditions other than gift-giving does the celebration include?

Teach: Review with students how to write a descriptive letter. The letters should clearly express the students' thoughts and feelings about one of the themes of Kwanzaa. Then read some poems to the class. Discuss poetry writing techniques and topics such as lyrical voice, alliteration, punctuation, poetic license, and similes. Provide paper for students to write the letters and poems.

Close: Display the letters and poems. Invite students from other classes to your classroom to read the poems and letters.

Assessment: Students should be able to write letters and poems that clearly convey their thoughts and feelings about the given topics.

Modification: English Language Learners having difficulty can express their thoughts and feelings through drawings. Students can also choose to do research on each celebration to present facts. This chart summarizes facts you might ask students to research.

Celebration	Country Origin	Official Language	Distance of Country's Capital from Your Home	Continent	Hemisphere (Eastern or Western)
Tet	Vietnam	Vietnamese	(Hanoi)	Asia	Eastern
Chinese New Year	China	Mandarin Cantonese	(Beijing, [Peking])	Asia	Eastern
Diwali	India	Hindi, English	(New Dehli)	Asia	Eastern
Hanukkah	Israel	Hebrew and Arabic	(Jerusalem)	Asia	Eastern
Kwanzaa	United States	English	(Washington, D.C.)	North America	Western

© Macmillan/McGraw-Hill

Activity **5**

Connection to Art

The Colors of Celebrations, page 46

Objective • Explore the concepts of absorbed and reflected colors.

Introduce: Ask, *What are the primary colors? Have you ever mixed paints in art class? What colors did you mix? What colors did you get?*

Teach: The colors we see depend on the primary colors of light that are either absorbed or reflected by the objects we see. Materials that reflect all colors appear white.

Close: Have students compare tables and discuss any differences they find.

Assessment: Students should be able to complete the table.

Modification: Have students use pieces of construction paper to create a display that demonstrates the information in the chart.

Answers:

Color	Celebration	Absorbed Color(s) of Light	Reflected Color(s) of Light
green	Kwanzaa	red, blue	green
red	Kwanzaa, July 4th, New Year, Tet	blue, green	red
blue	July 4th	red, green	blue
white	July 4th	none	all colors: red, blue, green
black	Kwanzaa	all colors: red, blue, green	none

Culminating Activity

Connection to Language Arts and Music

Design a Holiday, page 47

Objective • Design a holiday celebration that includes sound and light.

Introduce: Ask, *Can you think of an event that you would like to celebrate? What would it be? Why would you want to celebrate this event?*

Teach: Have students think about ways to mark the event that include sound and light. Have students break into pairs to work on original songs and music, costumes, decorations, determining the significance of colors, etc.

Close: Have groups present their holidays to the class.

Assessment: Students should be able to work together to create a new holiday.

Modification: Students can create a visual display that describes the holiday and explains the uses of sound and light.

© Macmillan/McGraw-Hill